WHAT'S WRONG WITH YOU?

What's Wrong with You?
How Natural Therapies Can Help

Dorothy Hall

NELSON

Thomas Nelson Australia
480 Latrobe Street Melbourne Australia 3000

First published 1984
Reprinted 1984
Copyright © Dorothy Hall 1984

Cataloguing in Publication data:

Hall, Dorothy (Dorothy Graeme).
    What's wrong with you?

    Bibliograply.
    Includes index
    ISBN 0 17 006074 8.

    1. Naturopathy, I. Title.

615.5'35

Typeset in Cheltenham Light by Galley Craft Communications, Melbourne
Printed in Hong Kong

Contents

Introduction

'Wholistic medicine', 'natural medicine' and 'alternative medicine': what do they mean? Does it just involve our taking vitamin C supplements, or are we to spend our time fasting and drinking carrot juice? Is it giving up coffee and alcohol, or is it jogging every morning? Is it meditation, or acupuncture, or bio-feedback or primal screaming? Or is it all (or none) of these?

There has been a recent wave of resistance at grass-roots level to the practice of technological, orthodox medicine. Patients resent its huge costs and depersonalised treatments, its drugs and their sometimes horrendous side effects so damaging to health. They are affronted by being reduced to a set of physical symptoms, and the loss of dignity and individuality they suffer. The swing towards simpler and less intrusive treatment of illness is world-wide, occurring even in countries which once were bitterly opposed to it academically. America has stopped sending its naturopaths to gaol! There is a flush of naturopathic group-practices setting up all over Britain. Germany has government registration. The World Health Organisation has issued reports recommending that Third World countries continue to use their native plants for medication, as they have done for centuries.

Enlightened health ministers are realising that home health care and preventative health care can save a country millions of dollars. Commonsense is returning to medicine.

Loadings break camel's backs if they're one straw too heavy: human patients often actually say to their practitioner, 'It was just the last straw, you know'; 'something snapped'; 'I couldn't take any more'. They are describing *stress*, that now fashionable excuse for almost any slowing-up in human endeavour. A better word would be *loading*. Everyone has his or her limit of endur-ance as Life's loads go on the back: the sad truth is that the loads humans are able to carry health-wise without cracking-up are becoming smaller and smaller. Our ability to handle Life's vicissi-tudes is becoming less and less. What a Roman army would take easily as a day's loading we would be physically, mentally and emotionally unable to do today.

Our Australian pioneers endured a fourteen-hour day of physical, mental and emotional loading that, five or six gener-ations later, would send us screaming to our Union reps, our psychiatrist, or 'up North' to get away from it all. Our individual personal stress is actually less: but our ability to handle *any* loading is diminishing.

Wholistic medicine, with its philosophies of health main-tenance and disease treatment, is really the ordinary, com-monsense medicine which has been practised for centuries. It combines knowledge of the natural sciences like biology, anat-omy and physiology, botany, meteorology and psychology, and that old fashioned duo of experience and horse-sense. It is based on accurate observation of *the rules which are there already*. Newer, man-made rules break down often: nature's rules, never!

I have written this book to explain both what this kind of medicine is, and what it is not. After around thirty years experi-ence I can now see the principles and practice of the art of medicine as deriving from a few simple, natural laws which are exhibited in highly individual ways. Breaking these fundamental laws causes illness and dis-ease. Knowing them and adhering to them results in true 'wholth' – true health.

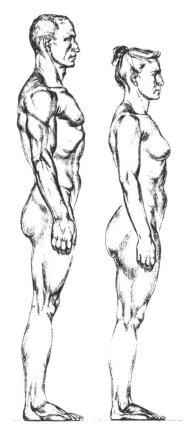

The complex structural and functional associated groups of specialised cells and their symbiotic relationships in one animal entity – Man. Divine? Scientific? or *Natural*? The practice of naturopathy is to understand the nature of Man, the needs, the breakdown of function called 'illness', as it is also related to the environment, the mind and the emotions.

1 *Hippocrates and Science*

Hippocrates was a herbalist. He was also an astoundingly good diagnostician by modern standards. His methods were entirely 'naturopathic' and could be used now (and often are in my college) to train student herbalists and naturopaths. Hippocrates taught a precept which today is sadly lacking in the mass-produced, machine-evaluated, scientific measuring of sick people: *observe* your patient. Listen to the details of his life; look at his posture, his gestures, the clarity of his eyes, the texture of his skin; *listen* to his story. 'If a man have a disease and be poor, do not charge him a fee and you have cured half his illness,' taught the master.

Is wholistic medicine, as it is called today, something new? Rubbish! It is as old as the hills, as old as the plants which formed the greater part of the early pharmacopoeias, as old as the 'temple sleeps' of the ancient Egyptians, when a sick man took various plants to induce a twilight doze, then talked to the priests and to Amon in order to shed his anxieties and fears.

Tranquillisers and psychiatrists are not new, either! The worries of ancient Egyptian farmers were no different from ours – taxes to pay, a sick child, an ungrateful son, a fear of poverty, a nagging wife – and it's all down in the precepts of Imhotep, the accumulated knowledge of physicians, surgeons, anatomists, embalmers, astronomers, priests and teachers of the art of medicine. They had no bio-feedback machines, no cardiographs or methods of double-blind trials with statistical validity, but their understanding of a simple principle of medicine made sense then as it makes sense today: different people need different foods and different medicines in vastly differing amounts; they need individual advice for different life-styles; and different treatments for the *same* disease.

Plants, like people, differ in their physiological chemistry according to environmental conditions – climate, soil, hours of sunshine and available moisture – even though they are botanically identical. Drugs derived from these plants reflect those differences. Dittany of Crete was preferred for medicinal use to the same plant grown in the Nile Delta. Olives from Thrace were very bitter, but two valleys away they grew with a higher oil content.

Centuries later, emergent science found this variability confusing, inexact and unpredictable (although skilled herbalists, who had always assumed that plants, like people, varied, had no difficulty) and herbal drugs were gradually rejected as science

'Medicine has for long possessed the qualities necessary to make a science. These are original observations and a known method according to which many valuable discoveries have been made over a long period of time. By such a method, too, the rest of the science will be discovered if anyone who is clever enough is versed in the observations of the past and makes these the starting point of his researches. If anyone should reject these and, casting them aside, endeavour to proceed by a new method and then assert that he has made a discovery, he has been and is being deceived.'

Much present othodox medical practice takes no account whatsoever of past remedies which still work today, or of past simple treatments which have produced effective results for centuries. Science 'discovers' *new* and clever things every day, and millions of health dollars later. Nature goes on and on producing the same, simple, predictable results as always.

began to produce statistically evaluative alternatives. To do this, science 'measured' the 'active principles' chemically in many plants. 'Ah; we can't find any statistically valid reasons for the other twenty-odd ingredients in *Digitalis purpurea*', announced the pharmacognosists, 'but two of its alkaloids do certain *measurable* things to a human heart. Therefore we'll call these the "active principles" and ignore the remainder.'

In this manner was born the science of pharmaceutical drugs. So-called active principles began to be extracted from thousands of plants, while the remainder of the plant's chemistry was ignored because of a lack of 'scientific proof' that these other ingredients had any effect on the human body. It was many decades before vitamins were discovered and trace minerals became accepted as essential and scientifically 'valid', proving that those once discarded ingredients were useful after all. Forty or more centuries after Imhotep's observations and empirical results, science is catching up!

Hippocrates has been credited with all the recorded teaching of that school of medicine known as Hippocratean, although his writing is now believed to be the collected wisdom of a group who followed his teaching and practical methods. In exhorting students about how to be a good *doctore* (translated as 'teacher', or 'one having skills acquired by practice in a certain field, which can then be taught to others') Hippocrates referred to several essential principles of medical practice.

The first, *observation*, has been mentioned. Observe and listen to what the patient can tell you. Look at skin colour, hair health, clothing and manner, and note it all down; look at hands and eyes and teeth. How straight-backed (or round-shouldered) is the sick person in front of you; is the patient voluble or withdrawn; old at thirty or sprightly at seventy? Such details are

'Furthermore, a clear and detailed record should be made of the patient's environment and living conditions, personal habits, previous surgery, if any, vaccinations and inoculations, and allergic episodes. In the case of sick infants, their feeding routine, and any history of chicken pox, measles, and other infectious diseases should be included. The general health history of the family should be taken also.'

Here is good naturopathy: recognising environmental and genetic factors as a contribution to illness.

often regarded now as irrelevant to a 'disease' state, or they are seen as the responsibility of some other medical department to treat as a separate and different complaint which has nothing to do with the symptoms at present complained of by the patient. They are, however, relevant in assessing the *whole* health condition of any one patient.

The second principle of naturopathy which diverges from scientific medicine is that *all* the symptoms and observed clues given by a sick person relate to the one disease pattern: the *whole* of the patient is sick.

So now we have two differences in philosophy and treatment between naturopathic practitioners and scientific doctors. Well-trained naturopaths believe that the same medically-named 'disease' will need different treatment in different patients because of unique reasons for an individual becoming ill that way. They also believe that a disease process doesn't only attack a throat, a left arm or even a stomach, but affects the entire body and its homeostasis balance, and therefore therapeutic treatment is required for the whole person.

Another Hippocratean precept is that of simplicity: employ the *least* intrusive and disturbing treatment so that the body can make its own corrective processes when disease becomes evident; and use simple language to reassure a patient and explain the 'disease', its causes and prognosis.

'Whoever treats of this art should treat of things which are familiar to the common people,' writes the Master. So much for Latinised medical terminology and seven-syllable words to describe a broken leg or a cold in the head! 'Scientific' medical terminology has been responsible for much of the mystique of medicine, the charismatic veneration for the doctor as a man or woman of learning and intelligence who knows what is meant by such difficult-sounding words as infective mononucleosis, Reiter's syndrome, epistaxis, and systemic lupus erythematosis! Surely such a learned academician must be only one step down from God! From mediaeval times the mystique has grown that if one has a knowledge of Latin and Greek which enables one to speak as the common man cannot, one *must* be able to cure all ills.

The Chinese 'barefoot doctors' have been amongst the most skilful of diagnosticians for many centuries. The textbook of their observations and treatments, clinical practice and advice, is a

classic medical document. Simple but highly accurate observations are made of the *whole* patient, and advice is of the most
commonsense, backyard fence kind, easily understood by
unschooled peasants.

Some years back I was invited to give a talk on matters
naturopathic to a group of medical administrators. At the end of
the two-hour session, one medical doctor rose languidly to his
feet, accused me of 'bad grammar', and announced that therefore
everything I had said should be discounted by the group because
of my obviously uneducated use of the word 'preventive', which
should have been 'preventative'!

I'm glad to say that such orthodox medical attitudes are now
in the minority! Patients are demanding much more information
about their medical conditions, their treatments and the
pharmaceutical agents used, their diets and their life styles. The
press prints long medical education articles in weekend newspapers; television programmes feature micro-surgery, kidney
transplants and endoscopy; radio programmes examine Nap-
oleon's haemorrhoids and Churchill's sleep patterns; and just
about everyone takes extra vitamin C when they have a cold—
without a doctor's prescription.

So the mystique of medicine is blowing away. The 'take these
tablets because I tell you to, and I'm the doctor' attitude is no
longer acceptable to most sick people, who have perhaps read
even more books on the subject of their diet, health and life-style
than has the authority-figure before them. *Commonsense*
medicine is in.

Do not think for a moment that some sort of war wages
between all naturopaths and the medical profession! Admittedly,
many to the far left of naturopathy hate and vilify all medical
doctors and technologists – and those on the far right of the
naturopathic world try to be as much like medical doctors as
possible. In fact, the latter group often advise replacing a handful
of medical and pharmaceutical tablets and potions each day with
an equally large (perhaps larger) handful of 'natural' supplements: this may be a swopping of therapeutic agents, but it
does not remove the underlying causes of the disease pattern.

A steadily increasing number of brand names on the many
combination-formula containers now available are beginning to
baffle health store customers, much as did the previously unintelligible names on pharmaceutical prescriptions. May I make a

plea to manufacturers? Keep your products *simple*, unless naturopathy is also to become an intellectually-elite zone, quite unintelligible to people who are earnestly seeking its help.

TREATMENT CHART

All dosages and durations should be re-tested as advised as these are likely to vary as progress is made by combined applications of treatments with diet.

SUPPLEMENTATION OF DEFICIENT MINERALS/VITAMINS THERAPY
DIET AND DIGESTANT

MATERIALS	DAILY DOSAGE	APPROX. DURATION
Zymo	One with every meal	8 weeks
Herbal Antibiodic	2 caps 3 x day taken with water or juice at end of meal. NO ALCOHOL to be taken within one hour before or after.	8 days
Hepagalen	8 drops 4 x day	14 days. Then change dosage or continue same for several weeks.
Minerals		
Calciumorotate	400 MG tablets 1-1/2 tab in a.m.	10 weeks
FAB 80	3 tabs daily (1 tab 3 x day) Then Dessicated Liver Tablets	2 bottles
Vitamins		
Thiamine (as in FAB 80)	After FAB 80 course continuous supplementation, or B1 may be advisable.	2 tablets daily at any time - 12 weeks
Folic Acid	2 x 25 mg tablets daily at any time	12 weeks
Choline A,B,Vitamins 250 gm capsule	2 x daily then 1 x daily?	12 weeks 1 cap 1-2 x daily
Quositol 250 gm capsule	3 daily 1 tab 3 x daily	10 weeks . (reduce)
B Complex 250 or 500 mg tabs	1500 mg per day Dose must be spread 2 tabs 3 x daily if 250 mg	10 weeks (reduce)

ALL VITAMIN AND MINERAL TREATMENTS TO BE TAKEN WITH DRINK, OR BEFORE OR AFTER MEAL

Very poor naturopathic treatment: a pseudo-orthodox list, complex and expensive, of 'natural' ingredients, to be taken as permanent supplementation.

Puzzled patients often complain to us of such complexity. They also bring in a shopping bag full of vials and tubes and packets and bottles and tip them out on the desk. 'Should I be taking all of these or more, or less, or what?' They throw their hands up in the air, beseeching us for the *simple* way again.

In the middle zone of naturopathy, are the 'people' people. Here you'll find no rigid rules and regimes, no 'Dr So-and-So's Diet' for everyone, or even for everyone with the same 'disease'. In this middle ground are the practitioners who say to you, 'Look, I'm limited in what I can do for your liver naturopathically if you're still drinking eight or ten beers during the afternoon followed by four or five brandies before dinner'. These commonsense folk explain to you that sure, you're drinking far too much coffee and sucking too many fags, and they explain in simple language what effect too much nicotine and caffeine will have on your adrenal glands as well as on your liver and your blood pressure.

They then advise simple replacements which you should take gradually: a pleasant-tasting dandelion-coffee substitute, not only easy on the liver but a positive liver tonic; rosehip tea-bags for mid-morning breaks or mid-afternoon slumps; increased vitamin B in simple forms to cope better with life's ups and downs (orange juice with a spoonful of brewer's yeast powder, a handful of nuts and raisins to nibble, rollmop herrings or mushrooms on wholemeal toast instead of steak-and-three-veg).

These changes are appetising and it is within any patient's ability to carry out the advice easily and enjoyably. Far better to be told this than to be subjected to strict prohibitions like 'Meat is terrible stuff that will rot your kidneys and constipate you' – only to find that the patient is suffering from diarrhoea and suffering no urinary damage whatsoever!

Rules, prohibitions, restrictions and dogma turn away many would-be explorers of matters naturopathic. The beliefs, rules and codes of an individual practitioner should not be forced on patients as 'the *only* way', when it is patently obvious there are different ways of gaining health and well-being for each one of us. I teach my students, 'Leave what's good for *you* and *your* life-style and beliefs outside the front door of the clinic each morning. What's good for the *patient's* lifestyle and well-being is what they are seeking from you.'

Hippocrates also taught that exercise, fresh air and water, and good food are part of man's health needs. He insisted that a lack of these environmental supports was a major factor contributing to the early stages of *all* disease. As global pollution rockets, it's becoming harder and harder to obtain the last three items. Exercise may not be *harder* to do, but our everyday tasks require less physical activity. Mechanical aids, labour-saving devices, motor cars, computers and 'space-age' technology costing billions of dollars, remove the necessity for physical exercise as part of our everyday load. You now have to plan time to exercise, set aside from your daily grind, rather than experience exercise as an integral part of every task.

'Blessed are the manual workers' may be another beatitude for the latter part of this century, 'for they burn off their residues while they work.'

> 'Whoever would study medicine aright must learn of the following subjects. First he must consider the effect of each of the seasons of the year and the differences between them. Secondly he must study the warm and cold winds . . . Then think of the soil, whether it be bare and waterless or thickly covered with vegetation and well-watered . . . Lastly consider the life of the inhabitants themselves; are they heavy drinkers and eaters and consequently unable to stand fatigue or, being fond of work and exercise, eat wisely but drink sparely? . . . Thus he would not be at a loss to treat the diseases to which the inhabitants are liable, nor would he make mistakes as he would certainly do had he not thought about these things beforehand.'

A third difference now arises between naturopathy à la Hippocrates and orthodox or scientific medicine: what you do, think, feel, say, don't say; what you eat and drink; what you work at; what your emotional state is – or is not – all these are not only part of your reasons for being sick, but perhaps the *only* conditions needing 'treatment'.

2 *Naturopathic Signposts to Health*

NATUROPATHY recognises three components of disease states or states of indifferent health.

There is the circumstantial component, which can have as a trigger heavy work loads; postural stresses as a result of a saggy mattress, perhaps, or long hours behind the wheel of a car; fluorescent lighting; noisy neighbours; and so on.

The physical component could be caused by a football injury, a chill caught on a winter's afternoon, a bad oyster at lunch, a viral attack which succeeded in making you sick because you were bone-tired from moving house or overseas tripping, a dog-bite, surgery, spring pollens affecting your super-sensitive eyes and antrums.

Lastly, there is the emotional component, and let's look at what can provoke that. 'I *hate* this job but I'm staying on to get my superannuation '; 'I hate my wife but she's not going to take my kids and home away from me '; 'I'm lonely and sexually un-partnered but surely that's got nothing to do with my tension headaches '; 'I've got a sales-meeting this morning, but why should that affect my ulcer '; 'I resent what my mother/father/boss/etc. did to me thirty years ago, but that's not relevant to my gall-stones '. Recognise any of these?

Each of those three-way reasons for getting ill needs treatment and advice. Each requires some contribution to be made by the patient as well as the practitioner.

Find out why you get sick

Many patients become exceedingly dependent on their health advisers. At our own clinic, we try to make each patient self-supporting so that they can understand, monitor and treat their individual reasons for being not 'well'. This can be done quickly, easily, and immediately after some circumstance has produced dis-ease, long *before* such disease patterns become so well established and chronically fixed in place that the only possible treatment is by more acute and intrusive forms of medicine. If the physical symptoms only are treated, whether it be by scientific medicine or any other therapy, even the most optimistic prognosis is that about one-third of the possible disease-causing factors will be removed. Illnesses will return, or symptoms will need to be continually suppressed by pharmaceutical agents. The only recourse for the patient is to accept a set of limiting health conditions for life.

Middle-ground naturopaths seek quality of life for their patients. After all, most of us want to break even the best rules and habits occasionally. You reach for a Mars Bar, or you hold out your glass for champagne at your first grandchild's christening.

> Life is short, science is long; opportunity is elusive, experiment is dangerous, judgement is difficult. It is not enough for the physician to do what is necessary, but the patient and the attendants must do their part as well, and circumstances must be favourable . . . Accordingly, the place and season, the age of the patient and the nature of the disease must all be considered.

Fifty per cent, at least, of every illness is caused by conditions *outside* the physical. The patient must change circumstances and emotions, even attitudes of mind which are contributing to ill-health. 'Doctore' translates as 'teacher'! The practitioner needs to *teach*, and to explain the patient's own contributions to illness patterns.

That glass of wine offered at your best friend's homecoming dinner may be less harmful to you – and to those around you – if you drink it joyfully instead of brusquely refusing it with a diatribe on the evils of alcohol!

Mind you, if you drink *ten* glasses of wine at the same feast, that's quite a different story, but *small* 'sins' are committed by all human beings every day. Tolerance makes the world go round just as much as a combination Vit. B and C. A cream bun eaten in the full understanding that the small sin you've just committed is completely reversible by eating yoghurt and drinking chamomile tea later, or having only fresh fruit for dinner, is not a health hazard! What *is* a health hazard is the holier-than-thou attitude and the refusal to tolerate any fall from health grace!

Some of the most wholly-sick people I've had experience of treating have been what I call the self-immolators. How they suffer to maintain 'health'! And they believe that unless it's unpleasant, difficult, almost religious in self-denial and 'going-without' rules, you can't be really healthy. Their eventual stomach and bowel cancers, foul breath, green skin and miserable expression tell you volumes more! Quality of living – your smiles and giggles as well as your natural goat's milk yoghurt – is what real health is about.

Naturopathic treatment

Patients often complain initially that many treatments suggested by naturopaths are *too* simple. Surely, they say, 'curing' hepatitis in two weeks can't be as simple as taking extracts of alfalfa and dandelion, and perhaps some fenugreek tea. The point is, of course, that we are not curing a medically-named disease; we are merely making available the ordinary substances found in a healthy human liver and used by it. Once the body is supplied with these ingredients, which are essential for liver function, a return to normal function is the only way the organ can go, providing the emotional and circumstantial components are in balance.

A lack of certain chemical entities can cause the problem by making the liver vulnerable to viral attack. Supplying these in-gredients in simple, vegetable-extract form, means that the organ should be able to resume normal function quite quickly.

The *emotional* component of hepatitis – the liver feeling the chemical brunt of emotional editing, deprivation or suppression – is often present, or has been present for a vastly longer time than the duration of a viral proliferation. The *circumstantial* component – heroin addiction, alcoholism, diabetes, poor A and D vitamin intake, or a thousand other contributory circumstances – must also be treated. There is no magic naturopathic pill for treating hepatitis, nor are alfalfa and dandelion combinations the whole story. Different causes require different methods of treatment; therapy and medication will vary according to the individual patient.

After all, what does the word 'hepatitis' mean? Just that your liver is not healthy enough to cope with an extra loading of *any* sort. One last beer too many during an argument with your spouse can make you awfully vulnerable to anything else nudging your liver, even a small load like a virus passing by it. That virus has been cruising around in you for months – perhaps years – without making you sick.

Viruses, bacteria, bacilli, pollens, pollution and food additives are with all of us, all the time. What precipitates them into producing symptoms of illness in one person and not in another? Whereas the dietary intake of all the right foods may be identical, one should take a long look at an individual's emotions and circumstances! That three-way connection can flatten in no time!

Chemical composition of Dandelion

'Choline, bitter material, 15.6% starch, which at prolonged storage changes into (fruit sugar) fructose. Saponin (according to Kroeber), fat, enzyme, traces of volatile oil, wax, mucilage, (gummy sugar substance) glycoside, 4.5% albumen, laevulin, taraxin.

The leaves contain inositol.

The fresh herb has a high content of potassium (K) and other mineral salts, calcium (Ca), manganese (Mn), sodium (Na), sulphur (S), silicic acid = Silica (Si) and a high(ly effective) vitamin content (Abderhalden).

The contents vary with the seasons. According to Wasicky the inulin content moves from 1.5% to 40% between spring and autumn. In spring the fresh root contains 17 to 20% sugar and laevulin. In autumn the milky sap becomes inulin. The milky sap is an emulsion of albumen, gum, a waxy kind of material called taraxerin, and a bitter material taraxin. In spring the root is highest in bitter material (taraxin), in August it contains the most inulin, in September it is highest in taraxerin, in October it contains the most laevulin.

The composition of the ashes of roots and leaves varies considerably, according to Tirsch the ash-content of the root amounts to 7.8% in spring, and 5.5% in autumn.' Extract from *Heilkrauter and Arznie-pflanzen.*

Dandelion is a prime example for the changing contents of a plant during the different seasons and also for the importance of the time at which a plant is collected and contains the most healing agents.

Man has still to duplicate such a complete liver-formula! Herbs are far from 'simple', now doubting Science is unravelling their actual contents chemically!

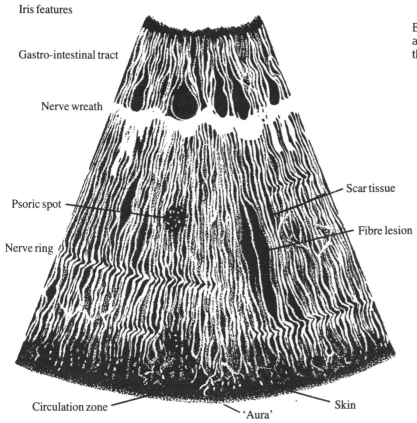

Iris features

Gastro-intestinal tract

Nerve wreath

Psoric spot

Nerve ring

Scar tissue

Fibre lesion

Circulation zone

'Aura'

Skin

Each bit of microscopic and gross anatomy and its function shows in the iris of the eye.

Iridology: a diagnostic aid

Orthodox medicine has recently subjected Iridology to careful scrutiny. Is it charlatanry, akin to reading tea cups, or a publicity stunt? Is it *scientific*? Does it perform well on double-blind trial testing? Is it going to be of use to the medical profession?

The answer to all these questions is 'No'. While scientific medicine continues to insist that psychiatrists and psychologists treat emotional problems; social workers and personnel consultants advise you on your job (or lack of one), and GPs and specialists treat every part of your body as a separately 'ill' section while the rest is going along fine, the tool of Iridology won't fit the job in hand. That 'hepatitis' liver may show no signs whatsoever in the liver zone of the iris. The problem could register in the jaw zone: have you bitten off for years those words you wanted to say but couldn't out of fear or guilt, or lack of confidence? It could register in your self-image zone (someone is consistently putting you down and you've resented it bitterly) or it could even be back-loaded to the liver from the gall-bladder, where an over-production of bile, say, can't be stored and bile pigments flood out, causing the jaundice-yellow of hepatitis. Resentment, brought to an explosive head, can cause this pattern on its own, without any viral horde marching across and through your liver!

Iridology is a very blunt-edged tool for those who think the causes of illness symptoms are restricted to physical structure and function interference only. As soon as science discovers what naturopaths know, which is that each bit of microscopic and gross anatomy and its function show in the iris of the eye in *three* ways, then the *whole* history and its print-out pattern visible in a person's irises can be much more effectively read and treated. It doesn't need a research foundation to establish that a heart can stop from overwhelming surgical 'shock' as easily, and by the same mechanism, as it can stop from overwhelming grief, or an aortic infarction due to cholesterol buildup and atheroma. That *same* sign can be recorded in the iris for all three aspects of the eventual heart failure result.

Science must rethink a lot of its findings, precepts and measurements when it applies them to such complex cellular symbiotic groups of associated specially-differentiated cell-types – or human beings. How's that for long words!

So now we find that apparently the greatest separation between Hippocrates (whose teaching we looked at in the previous chapter) and science is to be found in the *philosopy of disease* rather more than in its overall treatment.

The one natural law that never fails is that of balance. 'Whatever goes up must come down!' In illness the scale-pans swing out of control and fall off the balance arm. Therapeutic agents are needed to get the balance re-assembled. Teaching will be needed to avoid a recurrence. Day-to-day small changes must also be explained and left to the patient to accomplish.

In that same group of medical folk (one of whom chided me on my grammar) was an open-minded gentleman who was also open-mouthed when I spoke of the philosopy of homoeopathy, naturopathy, chiropractic, acupuncture, etc. 'Naturopathy', I postulated, 'states that a certain substance will produce a certain predictable effect in a human body. Too large an amount of the *same* substance will produce an exactly *opposite* effect in exactly the *same* part and function of the *same* body. Therefore, a glass of carrot juice is great for a human liver, with its vitamin A, iron, potassium, etc., etc. Twenty glasses of carrot juice every day will destroy that same liver.'

On I went: 'Homoeopathic philosophy states that a certain substance will produce certain specific symptoms as a 'proving' in a healthy human body. If a body be *sick* and showing all these same symptoms, that substance will 'cure', in various potencies for various people, those disease symptoms which are the same as it causes.' As an example, if a patient has burning, tingling heat in rheumatic fingers which are painful and cramped, and there is swelling and joint-articulation difficulty, then the homoeopathic remedy *Rhus tox* (poison ivy) can be given in small amounts because it produces a reaction like the symptoms experienced from contact with this plant. *Like cures like*. This is homoeopathic philosophy; the *same* cures the *same*, is naturopathic philosophy.

Before I could launch into the philosophy of chiropractic ('Structure governs function') or even that of the ortho-molecular nutritionists, many of whom are orthodox medical folk ('Fuel governs metabolism which governs homoeostasis. Allergic reactions to inappropriate foods cause disease'), this gentleman interrupted me with a question many of his classmates 'hear-hear'ed. 'What on earth has philosophy got to do with medicine?'

It's a good question to ponder. *Everything* to do with it, we finally concluded during a later discussion in the cafeteria. Without a philosophy one does not know the principle behind certain treatments for disease or one's reason for them. The logical progression from this conclusion led us to search for the 'philosophy of orthodox and scientific medicine'. By mid-afternoon, we eventually agreed that it went something like this: 'Scientific medicine *measures* many different body structures and functions, often with mechanical or chemical aids. If structures and functions fall outside the "normal" range the person is pronounced "sick" in this structure or function, which is then treated (but separately from the rest of the body) by many different means which don't necessarily aim to restore its original function. If a person's measurements fall *within* the "normal" range, the person is officially pronounced "not sick".'

We ran out of time before any of us worked out who it was who determined what normal range meant!

I didn't dare prolong our discussion by telling them of the many patients who have been pronounced 'normal' and who have then come to our clinic saying: 'I don't care if they say nothing's wrong. I feel terrible and I still have all sorts of demonstrable symptoms. I'm sick.' Those other contributors to disease, emotions and circumstances, may be the missing factors, but so may be that classification of what is a normal state.

One patient of mine springs to mind. A medical examination for life assurance purposes found that she had a consistently high blood pressure of $\frac{220+}{110+}$ at the age of 39. She demanded that I bring it down, otherwise she couldn't get a policy. Her health history was near perfect. No major illnesses or present symptoms, never a day off work, four healthy kids, a happy (and healthy!) husband, a 'weekend' farm where they grew vegetables and fruit, and where their free-range hens pecked the caterpillars off the produce, doing away with the need for sprays and fertilisers. Her irises were clear and brilliantly blue, and her major and minor circulation read off as near-perfect too. (So had the rest of her medical examination.)

'I could have been as sick as a dog all my life,' she moaned, 'but if my blood pressure was within "normal" range, I would have got that policy.' For her, that blood pressure reading was not only normal, but safe as well.

> Who says so? It's common that people *inside* 'normal' range for everything feel and are remarkably sick. Equally, as many people *outside* the 'normal' range have remarkably healthy, long lives. The truth is that every individual has an individual 'normal' range; *this* is what needs to be assessed and maintained.

Every person is different

The classification 'sick' or 'well' can only be determined by one person: the one inside the body concerned. That's why it is essential to treat every patient as a new set of rules waiting to be investigated. What is *their* optimum health pattern waiting to be discovered by Hippocrates and his mates, observing, questioning, digging and correlating; asking about finances and emotions and mothers-in-law and tight business-shirt collars as well as about asthma (which might be worse on Monday mornings or during weekends in the country at mother-in-law's place).

Each of us has a unique pattern which fits *no one* else; our health needs an individual approach, too. Why should you eat the same evening meal as your partner? Is it laziness, or lack of 'time' that has the cook doling out identical portions of the same items to totally different people at the same table? You wouldn't give budgie-seed to your cat or chopped rhubarb to your goldfish. Why should one assume that every human being has the same nutrient needs? Is skim milk powder really what starving Ugandans need? Is a macrobiotic diet as compatible with a western genetic history as it is with the cell-memory coding for the nutrient needs of generations of Asians? Are we all the same, as some ideologies would tell us, or do you still prefer – and need – to be *you* and not the man next door, or your own child, or even the man in the bed next to you in the cardiac ward?

Philosophy and theory always run the risk of wordiness at the expense of action. Let's see how to go about *doing* something. What to expect from a naturopathic consultation worries many people and prevents their finding out about the reality, but it's not as bad as you may imagine – depending, of course, on the practitioner of your choice! Do you want hellfire and spinach juice, or white coats and a quiet professional atmosphere; cushions on the floor and a 'rave' about health and stuff, or a brisk in-out-no-nonsense set of food charts and clearly stated instructions?

Just as orthodox medicine accommodates a wide variety of practitioner attitudes and training, so does naturopathy and its branches. I would be very wary of consulting a naturopath with so many diplomas, certificates of attendance and unsolicited testimonials on his or her walls that you begin to wonder how much actual experience has backed up all those obvious, confidence-boosting accolades. One worthwhile diploma gained after years of training at one college is often worth a multitude of 'Weekend Workshop in . . .' certificates. A specialist in *one* aspect of naturopathy is often a better-trained and more accurate diagnostician than the one who administers reflexology to your feet, checks your irises, manipulates your spine, massages your biceps and fits in some acupressure and acupuncture in the last ten minutes of your visit. (He or she may also advise you on your aura, your past lives and your present spiritual state!)

Whilst I'm not decrying any of these therapies, it's not possible to do *all* of them accurately and well in the time available for one consultation. Just as a medical practitioner may refer you to someone specialising in another area of medicine for different types of therapy or evaluation, a herbalist may recommend massage or chiropractic adjustment and vice versa. One naturopathic modality or speciality may not be able to fix all the problems that need fixing!

How to choose a naturopath

Look for professionalism from your chosen practitioner. Dirty fingernails and scruffy desk-tops are not necessarily 'natural'. I am always amazed by the number of people who believe all naturopaths will have bare feet, tangled hair and wear long black clothing, or at least look saintly in an other-worldly way! It seems to upset some of our patients who hear laughter from the clinic's dispensary and giggles from patients and herbalists in adjoining cubicles. Illness should be a *serious* business, they tell us. We should have long faces and a gloomy expression to reassure them that we know our business and are 'responsible' people. What's so irresponsible about happiness? Gloom, fear, depression and hopelessness kill more people than cancer – what a terrible set of examples we'd be of our own teachings!

So if you leave your naturopath with a grin and a light heart as well as your diet sheets and cod liver oil capsules, much of your 'therapy' has already begun. 'I feel better already, and I haven't taken anything yet' expresses a tribute to your naturopath (or to *any* health practitioner, for that matter), and to their professional training in what to say, do, see, and treat.

Expect to see some *results* from your treatment! I'm also astounded to hear stories like, 'I've been going to Mr Cureall for two years now. He's marvellous!'

'Then why are you still asking me to fix the problems with which you first consulted him so long ago?' is my reply.

If you're not getting anywhere, ask for a different area of naturopathy which may suit you better. Responsible naturopaths will recognise the need for a new look at the same problem, and happily refer you to associates. But what I call the 'Mercedes naturopaths' won't. I overheard one at a conference once, saying:

'She's my swimming pool. She'll be back twice a week for the next ten years.' Amongst *all* areas of the medical profession, medical and naturopathic, are those who fear that curing a patient's ills is bad for business! Over twelve thousand patients later, secretaries at our own horrendously busy clinic would be delighted to believe this was so!

Another side-issue often overlooked makes a naturopathic consultation a tax-payer's delight. Did you know that naturopathy (with the recent exclusion of chiropractic and acupuncture consultations) doesn't cost the government a cent? We naturopaths pay for our own research, our own equipment, and cover all medicine costs and overheads. We don't ask you to pay health insurance and then pay more taxes to cover the costs paid by government to cover what your health insurance didn't. Patients are usually charged on a time-plus-medication basis.

Give at least *one* practitioner at one time a chance to do a *complete* treatment. 'Too many cooks spoil the broth' was *not* one of Hippocrates' aphorisms, but well could have been. Six or seven different modalities, all applied unfinished, will only result in one conclusion: a confused patient and complete bewilderment as to which of the treatments, if any, has produced a result.

In our own clinic, visits are seldom more than at six-weekly intervals unless acute trauma needs monitoring. 'I've paid over ten thousand dollars to get my health fixed up,' one lady moaned to me, 'and for twenty dollars I've learned more about why I'm sick than in the last fifteen years.' Her shoulder 'rheumatics' turned out to be a chronically inflamed gall-bladder! Six weeks of treatment on all *three* aspects of her gall-bladder problem – emotional, circumstantial and physical – and her pain vanished, never to return. Needless to say, she sent along at least another dozen patients!

Choosing your naturopathic practitioner is exactly like choosing your medical one. If you try a visit, like what you see and hear, and the discussion and treatments make sense to you, give it a go – and then return for a second visit to discuss the results. I firmly believe that very few of the pharmaceutical drugs listed today would stay on the list if patients went back to their doctors and reported the results (or lack of them) from a course of such drugs. People, as people will, don't bother to return and say, 'Look, I feel worse! I came in with bronchitis, which is still there, and now I've got diarrhoea and headaches as well from those drugs you prescribed.'

Don't leave your doctor in the dark about what happened – or didn't happen!

Feedback is important

The same applies to your naturopath. *Try* what is prescribed; *carry out* the dietary adjustments or circumstantial changes recommended; *change* your office chair or your exercise pattern or your stilt-heeled shoes; *think* about how you got sick and the reasons behind it, and then *come back* to report your side of the story. It is a source of constant frustration to doctors and naturopaths alike that if you don't make that return visit, we never find out whether you haven't returned because everything's fixed and you're feeling fine, or because you've taken pharmaceutical tablets, or herbal or nutritional or homoeopathic remedies for a few days and then decided: 'It hasn't worked!' Neither naturopathy nor orthodox medicine can be effective unless the patient undertakes the treatment *as prescribed*.

'This can't possibly fix those chronic migraines I've had for eighteen years,' one former patient told me. 'One little brown bottle of herbs and an oddly-named herbal tea to drink before bedtime!'

'You'll never know until you've tried it, will you?' I countered.

He didn't take *any* of his mixture (we found out later from his wife who was a good and communicating patient as to her progress) and he then told everyone who would listen that herbal medicine doesn't work! Be fair with your health practitioner, orthodox or otherwise: judge on *results*, not on pre-conceived opinions.

Another patient came in with a list of symptoms and a regime of diet and exercise, positive thinking and meditation (which he said was what he had worked out he needed) and he wanted our approval to go ahead. Well, don't pay good money and waste time

Dear First-time Patient,

Now that you have had your diagnosis made and a herbal or homeopathic mixture prescribed, here are a few simple points to follow:–

1. The mixture should be taken in the "drops" dosage prescribed, in a little water. The amount of water is not critical. It is best **not** to add the drops to fruit juice, herbal teas or other drinks.

2. The dose may be taken **before** or **after** meals (or as prescribed) but **not with** meals or snacks. It is most effective half hour to one hour either side of eating or drinking.

3. If there are any effects from the mixture which you may find unusual or disturbing in any way, discontinue the mixture and phone your practitioner immediately. People react very differently and individually to any form of medication. Please let us then explain further the **different** experiences of Herbal Medicine.

4. Your **second** visit is most important. You think over our advice and analysis and perhaps remember important details which you'd overlooked: we can then at this second visit monitor your rate of progress and assess much more accurately how treatment is effectively changing your condition.

5. Please give us **at least 24 hours** notice of appointment cancellations. Your practitioner sets aside a whole hour for each appointment. If a cancellation must be made, this gives our office staff a chance to fill this appointment time with the many other sick people needing attention.

6. We do hope your experience of Naturopathic Medicine has been a good one and has made sound common sense to you.

DOROTHY HALL & ASSOCIATES.

Dorothy Hall

Statistical proofs of 'cure' are often demanded by Science from naturopathy. Here, both areas of medicine must rely on the *patient*. Tell your practitioner what's happened or not happened: don't tell only your family or the grocer! Only in this way can any form of medicine judge the effectiveness of its treatment.

asking professional advice if you want to do it *your* way only. Those years of training, experience and skill you're paying a professional for are all wasted if you want to make your own diagnosis and devise your own treatment.

It is certainly true that many patients *do* know, deep down, the real causes of their illness patterns and how to change their lives to avoid such stresses, but are reluctant – or afraid – to put their conclusions into practice. Sometimes, too, they prefer to take the advice of friends, neighbours, relatives or women's magazines, and they fail to get the desired result. For an objective view of what is needed, you should consult a professional. Those close to you are emotionally or physically – or even selfishly – concerned about how your illness symptoms should be re-arranged. They are in there with you, and cannot, or don't want to, see the picture from the outside.

Before you waste time, money and hopes trying every new diet for cellulite, every high-priced exercise plan, every vitamin from A to P, and a variety of minerals and supplements, go and get a professional assessment of your needs. That way you'll learn much more about yourself and your *individual* nutritional and circumstantial and emotional patterns. And only then, will you be able to help yourself, accurately and effectively. The professional has no too-close interest in whether your real need is to change jobs, countries, spouses or breakfast menus. He or she can only tell you how these things are affecting your health, and because of this, all must be brought to your notice.

The first visit is past. You have stuck to your treatment as closely as possible and returned to report progress. That second visit is the most important of all. You went home from your first visit after being treated by acupuncture and a massage, and smelling strangely but pleasantly of lavender and pine and oak-moss.

You have now thought about it all: during the first long, easy consultation (or a tight plan of diet-and-daily-dozen) you were told that there was evidence in your iris of an old lower-back injury and *at first* you said, 'Oh no, nothing like that!' But a day or two later you remembered the fall from your skis at nineteen, when you were flattened for three days in your ski-lodge dormitory, unable to move. *You* may have forgotten it – but your body hasn't. And what did you consult your naturopath about? A suspected chronic problem with your left kidney. And you fell on the left side did you? Yes, now I come to think of it. That return visit is a great education for practitioner and patient alike!

A lass came to see us about some small petechial haemorrhages which she had had around her face and neck for several years. (Let's call them tiny, broken veins just under the skin.) She'd had every conceivable treatment, orthodox and naturopathic, with little improvement. On her first visit she was nervous and somewhat monosyllabic, but luckily she took her medication religiously and came back to report. There was the same result: a little improvement. It was not until she was walking out the door that she said to me, 'You know you asked me about blood-pressure changes, or pressure or compression-type injuries, and I couldn't remember any? I've been a sky-diver for a few years. Would that have any bearing on it?'

'Come back in and sit down,' I sighed.

She now takes very high vitamin C and bioflavenoids, and vitamin K and Rutin, too, for the week before and during any sky-diving. The blood vessels no longer break down.

That 'thinking it over' space may also be necessary for you, as a patient, to ponder over what you didn't tell your naturopath, not because you'd forgotten about the injury, or didn't think some piece of informaton was relevant, but because you wanted to edit out details you thought might show you in a bad light!

One tough old silk-type iris gentleman, monosyllabic, physically-strong, impatient to get back to his job and the fastest writer of a cheque at the counter you ever saw, would zoom out the door after each visit with simple herbal medication for his 'dickey knee'. It took four separate visits, spaced over six months, before he admitted to his major problem on the fifth: a badly collapsed upper dorsal and cervical spine after a terrible fall from scaffolding years earlier – when, apparently, he had bumped alternate steel beams all the way down, according to what his iris had showed me.

At each visit I remarked on this and questioned him about it. On the fifth visit he waved his hand across the desk and said, 'Oh, that's all old stuff now; nothing wrong there. All over and done with!' His face reddened as I wrestled out of him the old ignominy of two years of hospital, a shoulder brace, pain and weakness. 'I'm as good as ever I was!' He began to thump the desk and raise his voice. 'There's nothing wrong now, nothing, except my dickey knee!'

Fifty per cent of naturopathic training is the same as that of medical students. Until the last few years, medical students at Australian universities received *one* nutrition lecture, and one quarto-sized sheet of information on vitamins, and I quote, 'Vitamin B deficiency causes pellagra'; 'Vitamin C deficiency causes scurvy'; 'there is no known physiological need for Vitamin E'! Who's 'uneducated'? Who's behind the times in 'past useless' information?

Your naturopath is not there to judge you as a person, only to improve your health, therefore you should never hold back information which may have a bearing on it because you feel you might be 'thought less of'.

Another five-visit patient told us that nothing had improved, leaving us baffled as to why there had been *no* change whatsoever in her condition, before writing a letter asking: 'Do you think alcohol could be gobbling all my vitamins?' A further paragraph disclosed 'one or two bottles of spirits *a day*' and compulsive eating of sweets and sugary biscuits in between times, as well as her medication. She had originally come in to lose weight! Be truthful with your health practitioner; you'll save money, time and trouble if you tell it all like it is at the beginning. This isn't a friend you're telling it all to; it's not even an acquaintance; and it's certainly not someone who will judge your soul, immortal or mortal: it's someone who must know all about you as accurately as possible in order to treat you accurately and achieve results.

The elimination process

Be aware that some of the health improvement you're looking for from a naturopath may need to begin with a period of treatment aimed at *un*-doing. It's not always possible to begin improvement straight away if there are residues in tissues, organs, the nervous system, even bowels, to be removed first.

One of the big differences between scientific medicine and naturopathy is this attention to the *past*, as well as to the present and the future. Naturopathy often aims to *un*-do and rearrange you physically and chemically first, in order to remove much accumulated rubbish.

At this stage of treatment, life can become downright uncomfortable! Your bowels may run riot on natural sources of iron and sulphur; your skin 'break out' as rubbish is pushed to the surface in lumps, blotches and spots by silica and vitamin A; you may sweat profusely; your liver wakes up on potassium, strange gurglings and churnings reverberate in stomach and intestines; and your respiratory tract begins to eliminate old mucus and tobacco residues, making you cough out all sorts of muck!

It sounds ghastly, doesn't it? If you would rather have all this still *inside* you, though, recovery and a return to really good health will be impossibly slow. As my grandmother was wont to say about all the processes of elimination: 'It's better out than in!'

After the undoing can come the energy improvement, the change in attitude to life, the understanding of future needs to maintain good health, and the real plus of good health – life becoming the 'experience of a lifetime'.

Persevere through any *un*-doing; the end result will be ten, twenty, a hundred times, more lasting and real. Sometimes new patients complain that their medication and new foods or dietary re-arrangement has made them 'sick'. On a closer look with them we find that only the processes of elimination are involved, and they are emptying rubbish-bin after rubbish-bin – not always a pleasant task! Some treatments can be stirring indeed! It's a wise naturopath who warns that you can't build good health on a clogged, slow, toxic-laden foundation.

Good herbs or bad poison?

Erroneous beliefs about herbal medicine are based on terribly exaggerated tales of the dangers of such plant-sources of vitamins, minerals, hormones, enzymes, proteins, starches and carbohydrates (for that is all they are, more concentrated packages of the same nutrients contained in your food). Much of the uninformed scientific horror at the practice of herbal medicine is based on this misunderstanding of the difference between a healing, beneficial process and a disease process with apparently similar symptoms. The difference is that you feel *worse* as each day of a disease process passes; you feel *better* and *better* each day as you sweat, or cough, or pass dark urine or foul, black faeces in that process familiar to naturopaths called 'elimination'.

'I got an attack of bronchitis,' said one lady after an iris examination revealed a heavily rubbish-laden brown area around lungs, bronchial tree and upper dorsal spine, and she had been given major expectorants and high-iron herbs.

'Did you feel sick,' she was asked, 'or have a temperature, lassitude, loss of appetite, headache?'

'No,' she answered. 'It was strange! I coughed up this dark mucus all day and I could hardly speak without coughing up more, but I felt more and more energetic every day. I ate well, and slept well, and I'm feeling even better now, although there's still a pile of tissues for me in every room in the house.'

She hadn't 'caught' bronchitis; her process of elimination had been safely concluded. At her next visit to the clinic she was given the *tonic* plants, foods and drinks for the same zones, now that the rubbish and remains of past sins had been removed. A fresh start was now possible. Bodies are astoundingly resilient if those two conditions are met: remove past residues before undertaking any repair work which is needed now so that good foundations can be laid for the future.

The dispensary in a consulting naturopath's clinic, where remedies are carefully mixed specifically for your particular ailments.

The herbs which are often mentioned by the knockers of herbal medicine (belladonna, hemlock, digitalis, opium, etc.) are those never used at all by modern consulting herbalists! Sure, the Borgias and their mates used herbal poisons (very similar to some found in the pharmacopoeias today) to remove the opposition or do some political re-shuffling, but now character assassination, not Deadly Nightshade, is employed! That old myth of 'poisons' and 'herbs' still inhibits some would-be patients when they look at their brown glass bottle of extracts and tinctures.

'It's almost exactly what the corner chemist would have mixed up for your parents and grandparents on prescription from the family GP' we reassure them.

Not so many years ago the pharmacist made up your doctor's laxative prescription from the contents of glass bottles and carboys of dark liquorice extract, cascara extract, senna pods and aloes. And those almost identical ingredients in our clinic dispensary, blended the same way for the same purpose, are a long way removed from black cats and cauldrons. It never ceases to amaze us all how long that popular folk memory of strange old ladies in long cloaks, their fingernails clawing the air as they dance and cackle round the pot, lingers!

Indeed, the shoe may be on the other foot, for those dangerous substances extracted singly from various plants remain in *medical* use! Atropine from belladonna; ephedrine from Ephedra; morphine, codeine and heroin from the opium poppy, digitalin and its related compounds from the foxglove; colchicine from colchicum, the pale autumn crocus; the list could be very long. All these highly-alkaloid plants can be dangerously toxic, depending on the quantities taken. Present day herbalists have discarded these plants together with that mediaeval reputation! Nine times out of ten, your naturopath will greet you in a white coat, and without eyes flashing red fire!

The process of going *back* before going forward to remove disease is part of every naturopathic treatment plan. One excellent chiropractor I know stands you in front of a mirror with one vertical line down its centre. 'See how uneven you've become side to side,' he points out. When he's feeling particularly ruthless about getting the message through, he adds horizontal lines one by one and you stand there, realising painfully what an ill-postured blob you have become! Of course, before that

NICHOLAS CULPEPER

Nicholas Culpeper's *Complete Herbal*, still available in facsimile today, was the first herbal available in English for the average person.

migraine history goes, before that anterior rotated left hip can allow your sciatic nerve some pain relief, before the dorsal segments of the spine relocate and give your asthma a pleasant surprise, you need *un*-doing.

The biochemist-naturopath has to *un*-do you first, too, after years of junk food and drinks, smoking, and emotional and circumstantial wallops. He can't give you a magic pill which will do it all – and he wouldn't, either, because bodies can't be fooled for long into thinking they're well when they're not. You may lose the obvious symptoms of disease and think you're now 'better', for many of the newest pharmaceutical drugs block off your body's realisation that all is far from well, even though you're still as sick as a dog and becoming chronically more so each day. Science can now give you drugs which not only block your brain's recognition of disease symptoms, but actually give you a feeling of well-being while you embark on the long, slow business of dying! Many children are put on such medication, even as toddlers, so that the lives in front of them will be blissfully ignorant of their body's chronically ill state. Dear old ladies come to our clinic with shopping bags full of diuretics, tranquillisers, heart starters and stoppers, pain-killers and sleeping pills; their daily intake is a chemical marvel of things to speed up then slow down almost every major bodily function. *Un*-doing a lifetime's dependence on pills or potions may be too much to ask of their bodies now, for they might not survive the withdrawal of substances which have become life-supporting. Therefore it is best that we start at the other end, with the child. Remember, every time you pop a pill into your child's mouth you're administering another part of a crutch which may leave their lifetime health permanently dependent on that crutch! Read, learn and ask whether there is some way of naturally *supporting* a deficient body function or organ until it can make use of the substances given it to restore normal function.

The greatest criticism of present-day medical schools in this country comes from the several million Australian patients who now visit a naturopathic practitioner of some kind. 'They're taught all about illness, some of these medics, but not about *health*,' said one silver-haired, twinkly lady of sixty-odd to me. In some medical schools, nutrition is an option — a few hours being thought all that is necessary!

Let's go back and listen to Hippocrates, who could have held his own, discoursing easily with today's chiropractors, herbalists, nutritionists, hydrotherapists and natural health societies. He spoke about exercise and fresh food, about emotional harmony, about circumstantial factors in disease, about the importance of *rest* when sick, about the benefits of special plants to hasten recovery, about sport and posture, about fasting, and about real recovery from illness.

His methods, and those of others like him, have been tested for thousands of years. He learned from *his* masters in Egypt at the schools around present-day Alexandria. The plants and the people showed the same reactions to each other in illness for thousands of years, even before Hippocrates; and Imhotep's teachings in ancient Egypt still make good naturopathic sense today. People everywhere laugh and weep, cough and sneeze, overeat, stay awake, have headaches and broken limbs, indigestion and anxiety; and they still need the same chemical packages in plants, foods and minerals in order to remove disease.

3   *The Body's Scaffolding*

OUR bony skeleton, the scaffolding of the body, is what distinguishes man from most of his animal cousins. Watch your cat, with its hind leg over its back and its head touching the tip of its tail, cleaning itself. Flexible isn't it! Yet humans must train rigorously for years to become circus performers, yoga adepts or ballet dancers, straining their bodies through pain barriers day after day to achieve another few centimetres through which limbs and spine can travel past a natural anatomical limit.

Worker ants can carry approximately twenty-four times their own weight of food or debris to and from their nests, without spinal collapse or 'arthritis' resulting. Even Mr Universe, rippling and bulging at around 100 kilos would have trouble lifting 2,400 kilos and carrying it three metres, let alone three kilometres, yet ants perform a comparable task many hundreds of times a day.

Compared with most wild animals, man's *structure* is the

weakest of all. Even apes have spines and limbs more flexible than ours. However, as man domesticates animals and breeds them for show or profit (larger size usually being one of the standards of excellence), their bony skeletons have to support more and more tissue weight and a lesson any structural engineer could teach us is ignored: too much weight for the scaffolding to carry and the structural members will show fatigue, if not collapse altogether.

Humans and highly-bred domestic and farm animals are susceptible to osteo-arthritis, osteo-porosis, spondylitis, and diseases involving disc degeneraton and wear. All these complaints are evidence of scaffolding which is not strong enough to carry out everyday tasks. Even standing up for an hour or more without moving can result in too much compression-loading on the skeleton for many of us! Feet and legs tire and demand a chair; one's back gives way and we *lie down* to rest. Many animals *stand up* to sleep, or at least sleep with the head erect and taking its share of the structural load. 'Go and put your head down,' we say to someone suffering exhaustion after even minimal or short-term physical effort.

Humans are now quite poorly equipped for bearing physical loads. But we can't entirely blame labour-saving devices, nor the incredibly complex tools which technology has provided for our use, for making us actually weaker. They may have made us lazier, perhaps, more reluctant to place a load on the structure if we don't absolutely have to. So where does this fairly recent human tiredness come from, that is, the physical tiredness, when our scaffolding is too weak to support us without crumbling, cracking, bending and compressing, and wears out at an ever earlier age?

Humans must train rigorously for years to become circus performers, straining their bodies through pain barriers day after day to achieve a few more centimetres through which limbs and spine can travel past a natural structural limit.

Strong bones and silica

Regular journeys to middle eastern countries have filled me with admiration for the physical strength and endurance of the hardy desert people, the Bedouin. Their bodies are enormously strong, yet they have a diet which many western nutritionists would consider below subsistence level! Their stamina and load-bearing capacities, however, are enormous. Even the women in their voluminous layers of thick black and brown woollen clothing stride, straight-backed, with their heavy and cumbersome folded goat's-hide tents to waiting trucks or camels, during the seasonal migrations.

The children with their tiny straight backs are a delight to watch as they carry the heavy stone jars of water on their heads, sometimes from kilometres away, back to the striped dark tent the group call home. Older children burden themselves with two heavy skin or black-rubber bags holding 20-30 litres of water each, yet they, too, walk easily (and without distress), laughing and waving to us, or sometimes proud, silent, and withdrawn as real desert tribes can be.

How do they accomplish what we cannot? We feed our children calcium and give them good food; some of us grew up in the days of the 'free school milk'. Our daily intake of calcium ought to be high enough to build strong bones and teeth and keep us fit and well, so why don't we have the strong, straight bodies, the perfect teeth, the healthy skin and the physical endurance of the Bedouin? A closer look at Arab people and their food-fuels will help us answer that!

Worker ants can carry approximately 24 times their own weight of food or debris to and from their nests without spinal collapse or arthritis resulting! Some humans have also trained themselves to lift enormous weights.

The silica-rich diet

Arab food can be very high in whole carbohydrates and protein. Grains, seeds, dried beans and lentils, chick-peas and almonds, are all easily transported and stored for a long time in the dry desert climate which ranges from great heat in the daytime to intense cold at night.

The way in which these seeds, grains and nuts are *prepared* makes part of the difference. Food for those people is essentially fuel only: fuel to keep energy high so that one may keep going. Every part of it is precious.

Traditional Bedouin grind their grains and seeds with the husks, stems and the grain-sheath intact. The roughage content, the iron and phosphorus is enormously high, but *one* mineral is found in the husks, sheaths and roughage which gives the clue to their efficient use of their bodies more than any other: silicon. The outer coverings of seeds and grains are loaded with it, and so are many of the highly-prized vegetables so relished in Arab countries: cucumbers, turnips and dates, grown in oases and by rivers, and pickled, dried or eaten with oil and wine vinegar. The dates are boiled whole and made into a thick 'honey' which keeps for many months. (Bees are unknown in desert areas, and any honey referred to in Biblical or desert stories from these dry countries was date-honey.)

Animal protein is also available when a sheep or goat is killed; much of the skin, hair and even the bones are crunched and eaten from the cooking pot. All these are high in silica. Absolutely nothing edible is wasted!

Something else so obvious as to be overlooked by us exists for Arab desert tribes: constant exposure to *sand*. If you've been there you'll know it gets into everything! (Or think of a sandy beach on a very windy day.) Mouth, eyes and nostrils; food and drink, clothing, camera-lenses, typewriters, bed-sheets and beer: the fine gritty particles bombard you constantly. Silica – silicon dioxide – is force-fed to you whether you like it or not! It was not until comparatively late in the day that science recognised that silica, in conjunction with its calcium and phosphorus partners, contributes a vital element to our human scaffolding. This chemical hardens and increases the tensile-strength in the large bones of the limbs and the smaller but vital loadbearing and *compression*-bearing bones of the spine.

At Memphis, ancient Egyptian capital of the arts and sciences, date palms flourished amongst the Nile canals.

Our hands and feet, possibly the largest effort/load carriers we possess, are usually the first targets for 'arthritis'. The more you physically load a body which is low in silica, the faster its skeleton will wear out. Silica is to calcium phosphate (the largest chemical component of bones, teeth, and structural tissues) what carbon is to iron. High-tensile carbon-steel can be lighter in weight, smaller in section and more efficient under a sudden or unusually heavy loading than its same weight and size of ordinary iron.

The bones of our present generation and several previous ones are starting to make extra *size* compensate for less load-bearing ability. People are becoming taller and heavier, the geneticists tell us.

The average height and bodyweight of the Japanese, for instance, has increased steadily since World War II. So has their intake of western foods. The traditional foods of pre-war Japan were loaded with natural sources of sodium and silica – sodium for flexibility and agility of muscles and sinews; silica for endurance and strength. Post-war statistics now show the two leading diseases to be arthritis and cancer of the stomach; neither of these degenerative diseases were prevalent before silica went out and calcium on its own came in.

Without silica-rich foods in our diet, we are going to grow increasingly larger, heavier, and weaker, until our bodies will collapse with alarming suddenness under physical loading. Those science fiction films where a huge blob of intelligence spends all its life in a chair unable to do anything but think and press buttons may not be all that far away!

If you are interested in ancient history, perhaps you've marvelled at the Roman campaigns, Alexander's conquests or Assyrian battles which took months of incredible physical endurance. Have you also wondered why we can't accomplish similar feats today? Out from Damascus in Syria lies the Krak des Chevaliers, a massive Crusader castle on top of a hill which commands a view over four countries. It was hewn and built of solid limestone blocks in twelve years by only several hundred men – no slaves. Present-day Syrians took over ten years even to restore some of the damaged stonework, using all manner of heavy equipment and tools. Is history telling us something? Yes! The decreasing amount of *roughage* in our bland, processed, packaged western diet has resulted in a massive loss of formerly available silica.

It is our choice: 'easy' food (easy to chew, quick to prepare, little to excrete) or high-energy food (harder to chew, longer preparation – in some cases much less if the food is eaten raw – and more excretion to stimulate our lazy bowels into stronger elimination patterns). We can choose between possessing physical strength and the ability to tolerate loading, or suffering a tendency towards ever earlier arthritis.

Avoiding arthritis may be as simple as buying a grain-grinder and making your own muesli from *whole*-grains, sheaths, husks and all; using tahini (ground up whole sesame seeds, almonds and other seed foods) on our bread instead of butter or the most newly-advertised polyunsaturated spread; cooking highly nutritional loaves, cakes, pastry shells, biscuits, etc. using flour containing *all* the grain, not just the soft central, carbohydrate part; buying (or writing!) a book on, say, *One Hundred Ways to Serve Turnips*; consulting food lists for those other vegetables and fruits high in silica.

Oh, and another piece of desert wisdom for you: Bedouin very seldom drink straight milk! In the dry, hot air it very quickly turns

The pillars in this structure are the skeleton of a building – covered by the outside 'skin' of stonework. Sheer strength of structure is still a factor in endurance and indomitability under many forms of illness. Potassium for muscles, calcium and phosphorus for bones, and silica for the hardening and toughening to carry loadings more easily; humans can be 'towers of strength' still.

into a curdled, yoghurt-type of separation between milk-solids and whey. Whatever naturally separates this way is eaten *that day*, and the thin, sodium-rich whey is also drunk, eliminating the need for storage or refrigeration. Their herds of sheep and goats move with the Bedouin about the country, so fresh whey and natural yoghurt is always available.

It can be most unrewarding to try the same separation process with our urban, 'civilised' milk. Not only are the cows from which it came having their own troubles standing up and staying alive for as long as their ancestors (they're approximately three or four times *larger* now and suffering, would you believe, from 'bovine arthritis'!), but as a matter of course they are given hormones and anti-biotics to increase their milk production and keep them alive longer on their degenerating scaffolding. Pasture grasses are certainly high in silica, as is all the grass family botanically, even asparagus, but this three-way partnership of silica, calcium and phosphorus can still be upset if the *calcium* component only is either emphasised, or depleted, as it is constantly in forced milk production.

Types of Joint

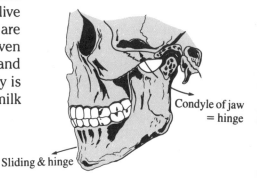

Condyle of jaw = hinge

Sliding & hinge

Arthritis

Can silica be used as a treatment for arthritic-type disease? Naturopathy has been using it for centuries. While *reversing* degenerative bone diseases can be quite a long undertaking, *halting* the process of degeneration will begin immediately silica is introduced in food or herbal extract or tea form, or as tissue-salt or homoeopathic tincture. Right from the word go, you will be able to carry your body weight plus its extra load of physical activities with a great deal more *real* structural strength, thus reducing the wear and tear in joints as bone grinds against bone, and the compression of the spinal vertebrae which occurs in even such a simple job as standing in the one spot for, say, an hour.

This 'wear-and-tear' of arthritic-type disease symptomatology can happen to the nicest people! Often I have told patients, 'Look, you may go straight to Heaven, if you insist on this kind of self-sacrificial overloading of your physical strength and energy, but you'll go in a spinal brace or a wheel-chair, and a lot earlier than you may have planned!'

Ball = head of femur, movable freely in socket

Our jaws use *hinged* and *sliding* joints to chew on food; other joints can be ball-socket joints which rotate. When silica is taken away from the diet, the same physical load you used to bear comfortably will begin to impose greater physical stress, causing bone-on-bone grinding and compression.

Arthritis is often labelled the 'nice people's disease'. As soon as silica is taken away from the diet, the *same* physical load you used to be able to do comfortably will begin to impose greater physical stress, causing bone-on-bone grinding and compression. Many so-called health workers in all medical fields explain to patients that arthritis is to be expected as part of the degeneration of advancing old-age. Not so, if early steps are taken to keep that balance of silica in there for calcium phosphate support.

Nice people often volunteer readily to take on the physical responsibilities of others – perhaps *too* readily. One patient, crippled in fingers, shoulders and feet and in dreadful pain still insists, at sixty-odd, on 'looking after her poor old pensioners'. She does washing, bakes and cooks goodies, takes them flowers, and chats to 'cheer them up', she says. She's going to need *massive* silica support to cope with what she loves doing, for she won't stop, but her activities are causing acute stress to her scaffolding and increasing its rate of arthritic degeneration.

The Chinese share two characteristics with the Arab nations: a tremendous capacity for physical work and thick, strong hair. The ancient Chinese penchant for long fingernails has a silica correlation, too: much of the body's silica is stored in finger and toenails, as it is in hair. The wiser and stronger the man, the more abundant the hair and the length of the fingernails. Symbolic? No! Nature gives us countless pointers towards her laws of balance. Sage tea, beloved by Chinese 'sages', is laden with silica. It's found not only in the structure of the bones, teeth, skin and hair, but in the nerve sheaths which surround nerve fibres and protect their nerve messages from becoming weakened or garbled along the wires. It is not all structural, but your nervous system carries the load and 'stress' of many nerve messages buzzing along busy communication channels hour after hour more efficiently if that 'hardened' structure is present.

Tough; resilient; energetic; these are the words we use to describe silica-rich people. If you begin taking enough of this mineral early enough in life, you have a good chance of *avoiding* arthritis of the skeleton.

But if your fingers are already swollen at the joints and the bone-aches have you in a vice, you can at least prevent further deterioration by taking aboard foods and supplements rich in silica, calcium and phosphorus, *in balance*.

Osteo-porosis

Osteo-porosis is a different outcome of the above problem of mineral balance. In this, the body's combined calcium and phosphorus are almost as low as the silica! Bones literally *crumble*, instead of merely wearing at load-bearing points. The same three minerals all need massive support. Unfortunately, the cortizone-type pharmaceutical drugs used to lessen the pain of osteo-arthritis have the unwanted side effects of producing osteo-porosis. You don't wear out – you disintegrate!

If you have spent time on cortizone and related compounds, you should be aware that you'll need support from the above three minerals, preferably through eating simple foods that contain all three, or taking simple supplements which support the metabolism of all three.

Cow's milk and allergies

That crippling bone disease, rickets, is now almost eradicated in 'civilised' countries, science tells us. Maybe so. Today's young mothers are certainly more aware of the need for sunlight on a child's skin so that its body can manufacture (via vitamin D, and its partners, vitamin A and calcium) calciferol and other associated calcium compounds essential for building healthy bones.

Cow's milk has been credited with much of the praise for overcoming rickets; and, certainly, at the time when it *was* on the wane, cow's milk was more wholesome and concentrated even though it was unpasteurised and unhomogenised. Many young mothers, however, find that straight cow's milk gives their children asthma, 'allergies' and digestive disorders. Why not take a middle course with a child by supplementing an ordinary, calcium-rich diet with simple Cod Liver Oil? The high concentration of vitamins A and D supports whatever calcium is in the diet and renders it more readily absorbed.

Distraught mums of asthmatic and 'allergic' children have noticed an amazing difference once whole cow's milk is removed from the diet and replaced by Cod Liver Oil and whey powder, and/or easily-digested natural yoghurt. Rickets may have been banished, but asthma and allergies now bedevil youngsters, who face a lifetime of pharmaceutical support for these (which appear to be afflicting increasing numbers of children) unless we take steps to discover what causes them, and then structure our children's diets to suit their needs.

Posture and arthritis

Bones may no longer *bend* as they did in childhood rickets, but how long is it since you stood up, really straight, to your full height, without needing to slump tiredly after *minutes*, rather than hours? Arthritis can also occur when chronic *bad posture* puts an abnormal strain on that same large skeleton. Chiropractic philosophy rationalises that if your skeleton is accurately placed in your body tissues in as near perfect alignment as possible, your ability to bear the everyday load of living (even lying down is just exchanging a vertical gravity load for a lesser horizontal one!) is more efficient and imposes less stress on the structure. Bones no longer restrict the freedom of blood vessels and nerves and the *need* for abnormal posture is lessened.

Theoretically, our bodies carry a load which is equally-balanced, side to side and fore and aft, but from the time we first walk upright as children we suffer strains imposed by compression and wear. If one part of the skeletal structure wears a little more quickly than another, we tend to compensate by changing *position* in order to balance the structurally weaker spot, and our first bad postural habits begin.

In later life we continue to make these structural adjustments until we develop such obvious complaints as 'hair-dresser's back', 'tennis-elbow', 'gardener's-crouch', 'weight-lifter's neck' – all of which are exaggerated examples of a constant structural loading *always* at the same spot. Arthritis at such points is not only likely, but a foregone conclusion!

It's a wise cricketer who plays golf (preferably with his *other* hand!) and swims as well; it's a wise gardener who plays tennis. An architect who listens to his body's requirements plays squash at lunch-time after long hours bent over a drawing board. But if you carry bags of cement all day and then build yourself a cement house at the weekend, beware!

Change the focus of postural loadings frequently. Bend or stretch! If you've had your arms in front of you all day writing at an office desk, try backstroke swimming at night! Become aware of the positions you spend time in all day, then try to flex and bend

Age points showing!

Old age posture, with arthritis inevitably the outcome. Sagging tissues, tired muscles, ligaments and tendons stretched, weariness in every line. There is certainly a case for exercise and fitness routines well on in years. Active physical life should not end at 40, or even 30!

Someone who develops 'weight-lifter's neck' does so because of constant structural loadings *always* at the same spot.

yourself the *opposite* way when relaxing. This evens the score posturally and prevents you becoming a chiropractor's nightmare because you always apply the same load to the same part of your skeletal structure.

Children do this naturally, bending and flexing, jumping up and rolling over, tumbling and bouncing, for they are instinctively aware that their bodies need different postural experiences as much as they need to experience different foods and a multitude of facts so that they can sample *all* elements needed to maintain balance physically, mentally, emotionally and circumstantially and make choices from their experiences. Many arthritic folk never counter-balance their postural loadings, so that wear and tear is concentrated in the same movement at the same small zone of the body over and over again. What follows? Degeneration at this point, of course.

Helping fractures heal

Bone fractures can happen to all of us as a result of a moment's inattention or a hasty postural relocation which our body can't balance effectively, and so over we go! Almost all of these fractures are quick, and they also traumatise surrounding tissue.

The same triumvirate of minerals, calcium, phosphorus and silica, is required here too.

See how really simple good naturopathy can be? So often it is just a matter of giving the body the nutritional components which the tissue, organ or structure needs, then standing back to watch it repair itself. Certainly I'm not advocating the abolition of plaster casts or even crêpe support bandages, but fractures heal *faster* and in more accurate alignment if the mineral support is given. Calcium phosphate on its own is not enough. Without the silica, the healed bone will be *weaker* than before, and unable to carry its former structural load. This is the mineral most commonly left out, even in some naturopathic procedures, in the treatment of fractures.

If you've ever had a broken leg or arm, you will remember how you coddled it, even after it was pronounced fit again. You didn't put all your weight on that leg; or you didn't lift anything with the previously injured arm any more. Our instincts tell us it's not as strong as it used to be and because we 'favoured' it, as the older medical term says, all sorts of structural imbalances and postural re-alignments occurred as a consequence. If silica is added to the calcium phosphate (and another helper, vitamin C, which we'll look at later) this period of hesitancy is much shorter.

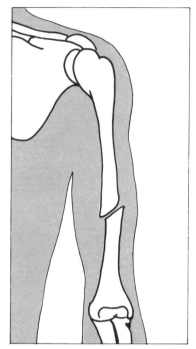

Simple fracture in arm; bone alignment after healing should be perfect again

As the break heals, it can then carry the same load as it did before (perhaps even more if you had low levels of silica in the first place!). If you don't add the silica, arthritis may very often occur at the site of the break or at the nearest load-bearing joint. Your structure at that point is no longer able to carry even normal loads, let alone an extra one.

Even a bruised bone can become arthritic. The damage may not be very painful, unless you knock it again, but bones feel 'shock', and small blood vessels are broken and bone cells damaged just as they are in a fracture – maybe more extensively. In the long run, hockey players' ankles are just as arthritis-prone as those motor bike crash victims with multiple fractures. Bad bruising to the bone can produce arthritis months or even years later, if those simple nutritional supports are not given at the time of convalescence.

Vitamin C and stress

Vitamin C, in its role as 'cement', can also help the skeletal structure by tightly bonding the new cells which form after damage caused by fractures or bruises or even after bone surgery, and maintaining structural strength as before. If vitamin C levels were previously too low, those bones may be even better than they were before the accident.

A third reason for the type of 'arthritis' which would be treated medically with cortizone and its associated compounds is when insufficient vitamin C is stored in the body. Two major storage tanks exist in the body for this vitamin, the adrenal glands and the eyes; high concentrations are found there when someone enjoys good health. Many of those hardworking, willing and helpful folk I mentioned previously use up *all* their stores of vitamin C in constant adrenally-draining activity all day, and sometimes half the night too! Such people are not only prone to arthritis, but to many of the eye symptoms associated with the different forms of arthritis (e.g. 'dry' eyes).

Because their adrenal glands lack reserves of vitamin C, their normal production of that ordinary human hormone, cortizone, is inhibited. Did you realise that in *good* adrenal health, our bodies manufacture cortizone as a natural protecton against many diseases of structure and function? Without sufficient vitamin C, we cannot do this adequately for our now larger frames.

Unless you lead an idyllic existence on a tropical island or mountain-top farm, eating *pure* fruit and vegetables grown in rich virgin soil, it is almost certain that you aren't getting even the amount of vitamin C that our grandparents found easily available to them from the produce of their backyard vegetable gardens and fruit trees.

Their arthritis resulted from physically exhausting lives of long hours of hard work, but the vitamin C available from fresh foods then was high. In our easier, less physically-demanding lifestyles, our depletion of adrenal gland vitamin C can stem from quite a different cause – what is often politely called 'stress' and is now being given the status of a 'disease' medically.

Stress is simply the 'load applied'. If your load is more than you can physically and emotionally bear, you could suffer from 'adrenal depletion arthritis' unless you take early steps to avoid it. Add supplements of vitamin C regularly to your diet, especially if you drink and smoke, for both the latter will drain those adrenal storage tanks! Drink your rosehip tea and eat your grapefruit; use

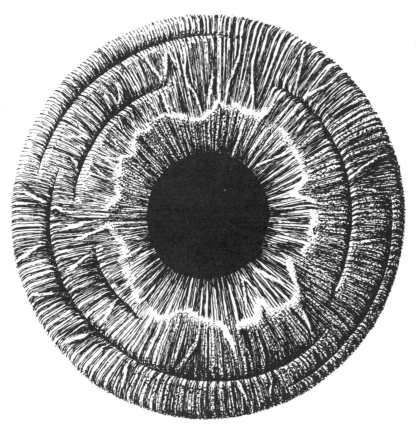

Iris, showing nerve wreath. When muscular tension is high and constant, 'echo' ripples of nerve rings register concentrically outside the nerve wreath.

lemons, grated rind and all, every day in cooking. (The *Natural Health Book* and *Natural Health Cookbook* tell you how.)

Take *larger* amounts of vitamin C if your life has been tougher than usual and you're feeling anxious, exhausted, and lacking the strength to fight back. 'I'm over-loaded', one says in despair. True, and if you are the arthritis-prone type, you will be well on the way to beating those bone aches, if you take steps *now*!

One other activity depletes those adrenal storage tanks: anxiety. 'Fear' would be a more honest word for it! If you worry constantly about all sorts of experiences, large and small, every-day or unusual, you run the risk of losing some of your natural cortizone protection against arthritis, for adrenalin is used up faster when fears are high. If you stop worrying and *do* something about solving those worrisome situations, your susceptibility to arthritis declines. You're using cortizone and adrenalin as they were meant to be used in good health – to fight a good fight, resolve the difficulty and remove your fears.

Alleviating bone disease

If we look at that list of biochemic necessities for bones and for helping our structure and framework cope with movement and loading, we see it is quite a short one. Calcium, phosphorus, silica and vitamin C between them will alleviate most of the medically-named diseases affecting the skeleton. Even exotic complaints like tuberculosis of the bones, gonorrheal arthritis, 'stunted' growth diseases where bone epipheses don't activate properly, and an endless list of 'syndromes' affecting the skeleton, can all be gradually stimulated towards better function and more normal structure if you have an adequate intake of those basic ingredients.

Sometimes organic iron is added to improve the function of those blood vessels in the bone; sometimes magnesium helps the phosphorus enhance the nerves' ability to keep those messages coming and lessen the *pain* associated with bone disease.

Muscles, ligaments and joints

It's hard to be an effective chiropractor if soft tissue and muscle structures are not massaged *before* adjusting the bones! And when bones are to be snapped around into different spots it is also much more painful for the patient if tense, tight muscle bundles are already holding the bones in the 'wrong' spot. You may have experienced this when resistant muscles and attachments refused to 'let go' while your chiropractor sweated and asked you to 'relax'.

Osteopathic procedures include muscle and ligament attention as part of your structural re-alignment. Most chiropractors are not aware that it's easier on patient and practitioner if muscles flop, and attachments, ropey ligaments and 'gristle' are not grimly tight and taut.

Flexibility

Have you ever tried to pull the 'gristle' away from the joint of a baked leg or shoulder of lamb? A round, strong, semi-transparent 'cable' holds against bone and joint and this contracts and tightens under roasting heat. Without these immensely strong and bulky 'ropes', 'cables' and 'supports', your skeleton, strong though the bones may be, would collapse in a heap when you took even one step, or lifted your head off the pillow in the morning! A compensating system of immense flexibility and strength enables the skeleton to change position and then re-locate itself *accurately* again afterwards.

Those unfortunate sufferers from a disease called muscular dystrophy know the phenomenal effort required even to raise the head or sit up in a chair when muscles are pathologically weak. If one keeps muscle structures strong, less physical effort needs to be employed and less *energy* is used to maintain structural movements and balance all day. Efficient use of muscles depends not only on adrenalin, blood flow and pressure, and adequate nerve supply, but also on combined magnesium, phosphorus and potassium.

The 'cables' that bind and support your muscle-structure to bones. Without resilience in these strong elastic 'ropes' of tissue, muscles and bones would fall about in all directions every time a movement was made, and more important still, would not snap back into their right postural position afterwards.

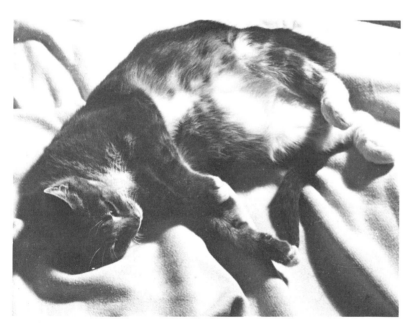

The cat is a master of 'flop'! A human who grips the armchair, neck taut and feet tapping, is *not* relaxing physically. Tension is still present in all the cables just as if you were running around the block. You may, however, be *mentally* relaxed. Both processes are different.

Relaxation should follow contraction

Not only does magnesium phosphate control the muscles' ability to contract and potassium determine how strongly that contraction can be applied as loads grow heavier, but magnesium phosphate also governs the ability of the muscles to relax again completely after the load/effort has ceased.

Many really strong people, who delight in sport and an active, vigorous life-style, or who work at physically demanding jobs, can't dampen down their activity levels enough to relax or even go to sleep easily. Their muscles are saturated with the acid waste products of all that work and activity; their bloodstream may also be struggling with an excess of uric acid after effort (or after the wrong kind of food-fuel for that kind of effort), and their magnesium and potassium levels are not high enough to render physical activity a pleasure, rather than a burden. 'Rheumatoid' or 'muscular' types of arthritis lie ahead for such folk. *Too* much effort; *too* much constant, ready-to-race muscle contraction; *too* much work and no play makes Jack, or Jill, not only dull company but potentially rheumaticky!

This certainly does *not* mean that a progress from bed to armchair to motor car to desk in the morning and back again in reverse order at night is the best way to avoid rheumatoid arthritis. Quite the contrary! But it does mean that the ability to *flop*, every muscle released from effort/contraction, should be achievable by all of us as one of nature's built-in balance mechanisms.

If you can't relieve this tension, even while you are asleep, your 'sleep' is equivalent in rest value to an all-night marathon! No wonder you're exhausted when you wake up and it takes you longer to get started, with greater will power being required each morning to do the same tasks! It won't be long before the tell-tale white, foggy, circle-segment appears at the top (or bottom) of your irises and joins up into a complete 'calcium ring' over the next ten to fifteen years. Long before you expect rheumatism as your genetic heritage ('my mother and grandmother both had it,' you say?), taking steps to increase your muscles' ability to *relax* as well as *contract* should help you avoid even the probability of such a fate.

Treating rheumatoid arthritis

The herbal treatments given to sufferers from rheumatoid arthritis include plants high in magnesium and potassium: celery, kelp, juniper, valerian, garlic, dandelion, and many others. Each has specific combinations of these minerals, with other vitamin and mineral contents supporting these two, from which can be chosen the most appropriate and accurately indicated treatment.

If you have this ancestry (or even the first faint 'calcium ring' shadow in your irises at thirty, long before actual symptoms are noticed), it would be advisable to avoid the possibility altogether by taking either supplements or foods high in magnesium and potassium *all* your life. If you have a 'thing' about celery, or you crave tomatoes; if hot milk puts you more quickly to sleep; if you're a little slower in the morning than you were last year and much slower than the year before; or if you toss and turn for hours

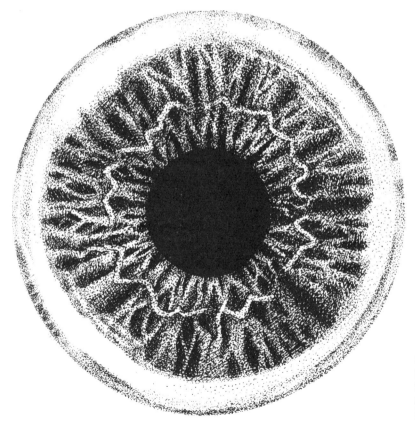

Calcium Rings in iris show an early tendency to structure rigidity, and towards arterio- and athero- sclerosis as circulatory calcium begins to deposit out in arteries.

and can't sleep because you don't feel physically tired enough, get in early to avoid rheumatism.

I recommend the same course if your blood pressure is higher than it should be, or if you can't relax in even the most comfortable armchair without feeling stiff and creaky when you rise, too!

Back pain

Muscular spasms in patients are hard on chiropractors' thumbs! While the patient may become accustomed to such chronic spasm, feeling only general pain ('I'm getting old and achy,' they say), these spasms can be the result of former or accidental trauma affecting the skeleton. The muscles pull and snap the bones all over the place with your every movement. Whether that skeleton is re-aligned accurately depends entirely on where your muscles and ligaments put it! Even lifting one finger can bring into action all sorts of elastic stretching and snapping back.

If this is not done absolutely correctly every time, the bones will stay where you've left them – slightly out of alignment. A good and honest chiropractor should admit to you that even as you get up from his adjustment table, you've undone all his hard work *unless* the muscle attachments and insertions and the muscles themselves are also 'worked-over'.

This is recognised by the comparatively new chiropractic advance into kineasthesiology. This study of the body's ability to contract and relax; to flex and straighten again, and to *move* – out and back in, up and back down – recognises both aspects of muscle movement (contracting and relaxing). It is a demonstrable way of showing the patient just where potential disease-producing tensions or weaknesses are sited, so that correction can be consciously applied.

The back is a prime unit where uneven alternation of muscular effort and relaxation produces structural collapse. Spondylitis is the inflammation and pain produced when muscle and ligament structures *clamp* the spine so tightly in position that *compression* and disc and vertebral wear result; often thickening and calcification in tissues occurs as well.

One of the people I admire greatly (and who is sick for the best and most praiseworthy reasons imaginable!) is a neurosurgeon. He faces seven and ten hour, or longer, stretches in the operating theatre locked into a single, balanced position doing the most delicate work re-threading nervous systems into perhaps massively-damaged tissue. His reconstructive surgery is widely praised, but the back pain he experiences in his job is excruciating.

The *locking* of the spine can also happen to those with heavy upper torsos, wide shoulders and big heads! 'Stand up *straight!*' is a frequent instruction to small children, soldiers and teenagers. Perhaps a better instruction would be, 'Stand up to your full height', or even 'Stand *taller!*" You can avoid spondylitis, if you're *not* a brain-surgeon, as simply as this!

Treating it *afterwards* involves another mineral: sodium. Organic compounds of sodium can improve flexibility and allow fluids to move through calcifying ligaments and rock-like muscle structures. Celery, already a rich source of potassium for tired muscles, is even richer in 'vegetable' sodium, and we use this common vegetable in a more highly concentrated extract, or tincture form for the treatment of many 'rigidity' diseases of structure. An added attraction of celery is that it also keeps calcium in suspension in body fluids, minimising deposition on and into soft tissues.

The higher blood-pressures which can result from muscular hypertension and spasmodic contraction of ligaments are often treated medically by potassium-based pharmaceutical drugs, or diuretics. The optimum balance of sodium and potassium is involved in *every* muscular movement. A naturally-balanced intake of both is also found in kelp. A simple supplement of celery and juniper tablets and perhaps kelp tablets (or, even better, use granulated kelp as a condiment on your table each day), can be a major contribution to your muscles' and ligaments' ability to contract and relax in a balanced way, as the various stimuli of tasks are applied and then removed.

Smooth muscle and spasmodic pain

So far we have been discussing *striated* muscle and its structural use. *Smooth* muscle is found in many organs, and it is also concerned with movement, with contracting and relaxing. The abdominal peristaltic movements which occur during eating and digestion; the stomach contracting and expanding in response to food stimuli; even the heart beating away at its 'on-off' contraction/relaxation pattern millions of times in a lifetime, are all part of the same story.

The same goes for uterine ligaments during pregnancy and childbirth, and period pains; colic and whooping cough, and some forms of asthma. The list could go on and on.

Celery is rich in 'vegetable' sodium, as is dried seaweed, olives, brown rice and dried figs.

Smooth muscle spasm and the spasmodic contraction of organs, is also a job for magnesium, phosphorus, calcium and potassium. One of the best, safest and all-round useful anti-spasmodics is just so ordinary, it is frequently overlooked. Chamomile, even chamomile tea, is just loaded with exactly what's needed: calcium phosphate, magnesium phosphate and potassium phosphate! Does that old-fashioned remedy for every-thing from writer's cramp to dysmenorrhoea begin to make a little more sense now? I like the continental courtesy of a cup of chamomile tea placed on the bedside table after you pick up your key from the hotel desk at the end of a full day. Many early stages of a disease pattern, if they are recognised and understood for what they are, can be treated by remarkably simple means.

One of my students, who was looking grey and miserable all through evening class, asked me afterwards: 'Have you anything for really strong period pain?' She'd tried everything: hormone therapy, relaxation classes, removal of her I.U.D., and a suc-cession of different contraceptive pills. She'd tried aspirin, hypnotherapy and acupuncture, chiropractic, massage and mind-dynamics. All produced only a slight improvement. Her irises showed the classic patterns of heavy nerve rings – con-stantly or acutely over-contracted muscles.

'Try some chamomile tea when you get home,' I told her.

'The pain went almost in the middle of the first cup,' she marvelled at next week's class. She drinks it often now, and has never had another period pain.

Chamomile, even chamomile tea, is loaded with calcium phosphate and potassium phosphate — just the remedy for anything from writer's cramp to period pains.

Over-active children

For many children, muscles and ligaments bounce and propel them about almost on spring-shoes, often much to the envy of their more tired parents! Many are classified (incorrectly) as 'hyperactive' on this basis alone! Take the jumping-jacks out of their shoes with chamomile tea, which young children often enjoy, although their parents may wrinkle up their noses at the sweet/bitter taste of it. These same children often tense up in abdominal and stomach cramps and are finicky eaters. Chamo-mile does the lot; *relaxing* such children can be a boon for parents and prevents these children developing more harmful muscular tension later in life.

Loose-limbed folk have problems, too!

So far the 'over-tight' have lots of treatment to choose from. But what about their opposites, the 'over-loose'? Chiropractors dread the hyper-flexible neck, the hyper-mobile shoulder, the dislocated wrist, the double-jointed fingers. For while there are lots of ways to *loosen* you up, *tightening* you can be more difficult!

If your bones click in and out; if your knees act like castanets even when getting out of a chair and you can crack your knuckles in and out of place to delight the kids, be warned! *Too loose* structure can also be a health hazard. As you snap and click around, the bone ends and joints are also banged and hit, and there is a high likelihood of damage in accidents caused by such loose structure.

To avoid this, many such people may lock into various positions to stabilise themselves. Although *compression* under loading is not their type, they often have to shrink a little and learn to hold on to their bones with their muscles somewhat more tightly than is arthritis-proof!

Rag-doll people, who loll about, draping themselves rather than sitting, can tighten up the loose elastic of ligaments and tendons by increasing foods containing vitamin E in their diets or taking supplements. Those chunky Olympic medal-winning Russians live on diets very much richer in everyday vitamin E than most of the rest of the world does.

Another good way to add snap and bounce to muscles is to eat a nutty-flavoured porridge made from a combination of millet and linseed grains, as a change from the high vitamin E of oats or buckwheat. Such a *simple* thing good health can be!

In winter, make thick porridge your daily starter, hot, comforting, filling and energy-packed, and collect those B and E vitamins, iron, phosphorus and so on from the grains used.

In warmer weather, a thinner porridge of millet and linseed meal is rich in all the same things but much lower in carbohydrate (though *higher* in much-needed protein!)

Your harder winter exercise, as well as the cold, will burn off the excess calories of the higher-carbohydrate oatmeal or wheat-

Eat porridge in summer and you put on weight. Eat porridge in winter and you burn it up in body-heating and more energetic activity. Of course, if you break Nature's rules and air-condition to chilly temperatures in summer, and warm to sultry heat your home in winter you break this natural law and *any* porridge-eating upsets your metabolism.

> 'Farinaceous food is most difficult to digest in summer and autumn, easiest in winter and next easiest in spring.'

meal porridge. Of course, a really easy business all year round is nutritionally-packed homemade muesli with these grains as a base.

Massage has therapeutic value

It's a shame that the regular massage of bodies seems to have been relegated to dubious houses with pink chiffon curtains advertised in the pages of Sunday newspapers, rather than to being written about in the 'health' section. Those aforementioned loose-limbed folk need not only the internal consumption of linseed, but a regular massage with linseed oil around joints and spine, particularly at the points where muscles are attached by strong ligamentous tissue to the bones of the skeleton. The raw, brownish linseed oil used by house-painters is best, and the hardware store can sell you the small quantity you need. Even a once-a-week 'lube' around hyper-flexible cracking joints should be enough; use it more often if the joint is weak or painful.

The side-benefit of this is that wrinkling of the skin can be minimised – although linseed oil is not recommended as a cosmetic for *all* wrinkles: you could finish up varnished, almost! These loose-limbed folk also tend to have loose skin which can over-stretch and hang in folds. My husband attributes his much-envied lack of wrinkles to the fact that over many years of training and work as artist, interior decorator, graphic designer, museum restoration artist, signwriter, and art-teacher, he cleaned off all the paint specks from hands, face and body with raw linseed oil at the end of each day. As he is one of the bodies with hyper-flexible ligaments, he quite unconsciously chose the best possible corrective treatment.

Most people know what's really good for them if they listen to that small, inner voice, instead of accepting any outside instructions – including mine – if they feel 'wrong'.

Treating sprains, torn ligaments and other trauma

Most of us have experienced acute trauma involving the mechanical function of joints, ligaments and muscles. Tears, sprains,

a Shoulder and upper back are always prone to poor posture or strain due to physical tasks or sporting activities.

b Arm and elbow also take much of the lifting and tension of daily tasks or job postures. Many industrial injuries involve arms and hands, and chiropractic adjustment after massage can help relieve such tension and pain.

c Lower spine and hips take the gravity-weight of the body. Standing for long periods in one spot can cause compression and postural mis-alignment in these zones, causing pain there and in legs.

d Neck tension often comes from
e dorsal-spine posture and mis-alignment, and can cause headaches, migraines etc.

f Neck stretching and upper-back and shoulder adjustment

g Lining-up posture and levels of hips. 'One side up and one side down' can cause all sorts of pains and aches in legs and thighs, and in lower back.

h Mid-dorsal checking for out-of-alignment vertebrae

i Mid-dorsal checking for out-of-alignment vertebrae

j The back is always the first place to look for spinal out-of-place vertebrae, which then cause pressure on nerves and occlusion of blood vessels in the zone affected.

k Final check of muscles which should now be relaxed, allowing bones to re-assume better position

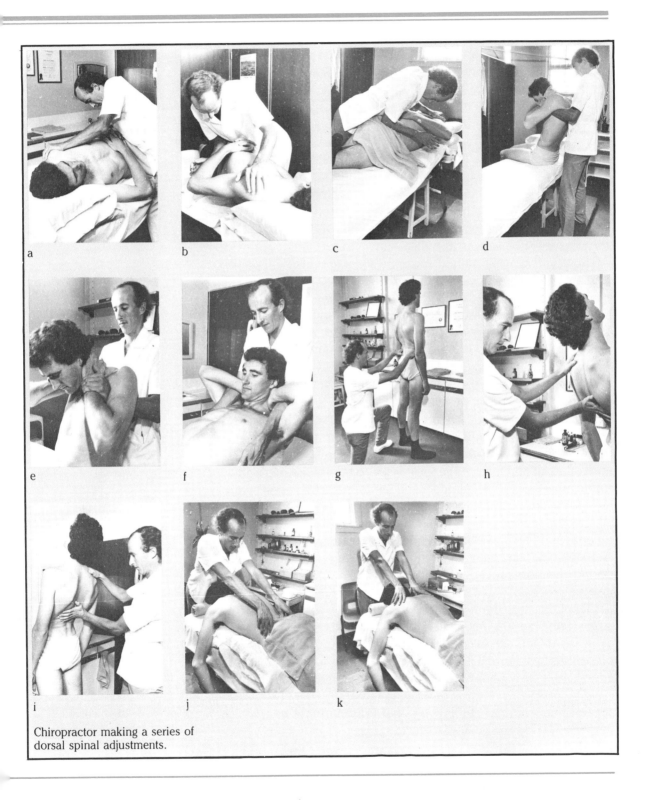

Chiropractor making a series of
dorsal spinal adjustments.

dislocations, strains and that newly important disease called tenosynovitis all cause sudden and acute pain as anatomic limits are passed once or many times. Chronic weakness and pain can be the result of these injuries also.

Fluid effusion from an injured joint or torn tissue is the body's way of immediately cushioning the damaged part, and this puffing-up effect of the fluid can also restrict the movement of a joint or a set of ligaments or tendons. Nature has many ways of informing us that we need rest and time in which to recuperate. Some of us neither listen nor learn, unfortunately! Putting weight or effort/loading on such an obviously traumatised zone is asking for permanent weakness and disability.

Sure, you can take painkillers, apply ice-packs, use will power and plead financial necessity as hurry-up tactics, but nature will have her lesson there for you to learn sometime. Your trips for physiotherapy and chiropractic adjustment, and the chemist's bills for analgesics may go on for years, whereas one or two more days' rest and a few simple home treatments could have prevented such long-term limitation of health.

Patience is the most-needed remedy for these acute traumas! And while you're being patient, apply two herbal agents: wintergreen oil massaged well into the affected part several times a day, and a witch-hazel lotion compress in between massages.

Witch-hazel is a highly-astringent plant which will minimise fluid effusion and encourage torn tissue to rejoin and heal; and, more importantly, the ligaments and tendons are tightened again to the condition they were before the injury.

The wintergreen oil is full of silica compounds to reduce inflammation and swelling, and it penetrates deeply, producing heat to minimise pain. Neither of these two agents by-pass normal healing procedures; all they do is safely hasten the healing process.

The third ingredient for healing, comfrey, may be taken in tablet form, as a few fresh green leaves in salad each day, as tea, or as an ingredient in a fluid mixture of tinctures or extracts prescribed by a herbalist. The alantoin it contains (which is also added to many pharmaceutical healing agents, ointments, creams, cosmetics, etc.) is best taken internally to increase the speed of new normal cell growth after the trauma of injury.

Comfrey contains the healing ingredient allantoin which is also added to many pharmaceutical healing agents.

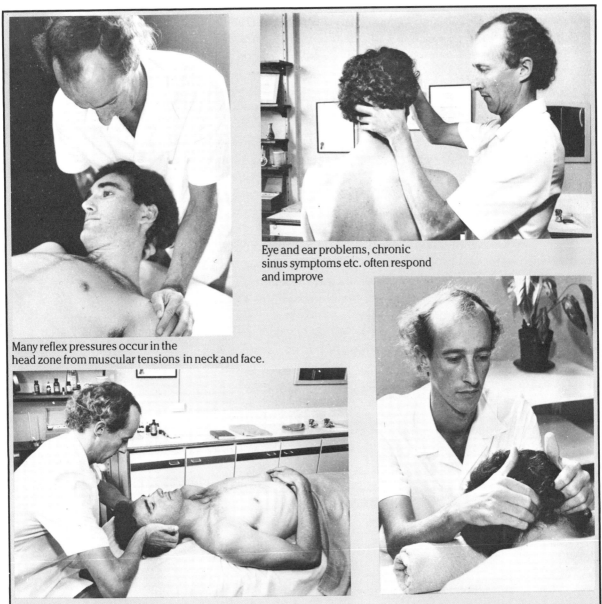

Eye and ear problems, chronic sinus symptoms etc. often respond and improve

Many reflex pressures occur in the head zone from muscular tensions in neck and face.

Neck vertebrae must move easily and well to avoid neuralgias and head and face tension and pain.

Jaw and mouth also respond well to cranial adjustment pressure

Tenosynovitis

Tenosynovitis, the new name for chronic tiring, weakening and inflammation of a set of ligaments resulting from the same repetitive movement, has surfaced on assembly lines in factories and in offices as increasing mechanisation forces humans to become extensions of machines. One way of preventing its

occurrence is to rotate each worker to a different machine re-
quiring the use of a different set of movements each day. Too
simple? Good health *can* be easy! Otherwise, if you're more
interested in fat bundles of worker's compensation money than in
good health and strength, don't use wintergreen oil, witch-hazel
or comfrey!

Exercise not only extends structural components to keep
them strong, but *changes* stress-loadings physically. The same
applies to ligaments and tendons as to muscles: don't go home
and knit at night in the armchair to relax if you sit all day in front of
a typewriter with your arms in exactly the same position and your
shoulders employing the same kind of tension on your arms via
the tendons.

After I've been writing non-stop for several hours I go out and
do the washing or vacuum-cleaning, to give a different part of the
'elastic' a stretch. Those school teachers who encourage their
classes to stretch, arms above heads, backs flexed and arched,
and joggle their heads around for a few minutes understand the
stresses of study better than those who demand perfect stillness
in one position for long hours of 'paying attention'. Paying is the
word! The body elastic gets more tired in one position only than it
ever does in continually changing movement.

Exercise different pieces of your 'elastic' all day. Change
positions, tasks and loadings often!

You're stuck with your scaffolding. It's your vehicle to drive in
through life and, like all mechanical moving parts, it needs
maintenance. Include a regular massage in your weekly programme. Sportspeople do it: they know the essentials for fine
performance.

If you are content to trundle about in an old, broken-down,
poorly-maintained, rust-bucket of a motor car, perhaps you
haven't realised that your body can look and perform in the same
uncared-for way.

On the other hand, if you have regular grease-and-oil changes
and services on your vehicle, it performs much more efficiently.
You may keep priding yourself that you can take it! Well, if you
expect your old age to consist of years of misery paying for the
carelessness of your youth, then you'll certainly find it to be true!
There's no need to expect your body to degenerate rapidly if
constant minimal maintenance is supplied throughout your life.

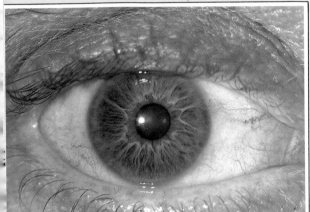

Right iris

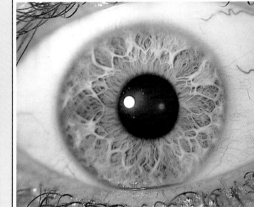

Left iris

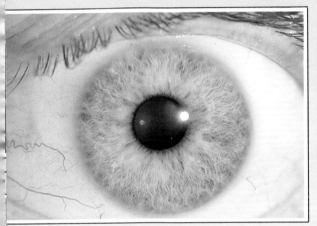

Right iris

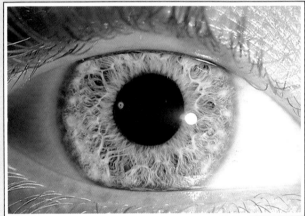

Right iris

hyperactive-type irises. So-called hyperactive people can
burn themselves out. 'Earth' yourself – garden in your spare
time, walk barefoot on a lonely beach, have a massage with
someone else's hands and gentle oils against the skin

The Band of the Welsh Guards, the Household
Brigade (*top*). Black and red, the warlike colours,
and the shine of the brass instruments: the sounds
stir the adrenals to march into battle!

Elecampagne (*Inula helenium*) is rich in inulin, a muscle
sugar. Your lungs will be more efficient bellows when this
plant is prescribed for you (*lower right*)

4 *The Human Computer — the Nervous System*

THE human computer has received much more attention since technology gave us the mechanical one. Frankenstein's monster, responding to input signals with output actions, was dangled before us as our fate once the computer replaced us in efficiency, logic and long life. The reverse has happened. Computer designers are only beginning to realise that while speed of function and data retention can be computers' obvious strongpoints, some functions of the human brain still appear to be impossible to duplicate. Science has had to admit that nature is one step ahead – as usual!

Any text book will describe the anatomy and function of the human nervous system for you. One of the clearest and simplest I've found is the Penguin *Medical Encyclopaedia*, a small paperback containing practical explanations of the human condition. So let's look more deeply, past the mechanical aspects, on to the intricacies of our communications network and how it can make us sick. We'll take the household electricity supply as a comparison:

1   If the main supply is not connected, no amount of switching on will produce power.

2   If circuits are overloaded past their capacity, a fuse will blow and power will be cut off.

3   If not earthed, random electricity can kill or shock.

4   Never use 5 amp wire in a 30 amp circuit.

5   Wires must be insulated from each other, otherwise a short circuit may blow the whole system. Static and poor signals are received electrically when wires are not well insulated.

6   Leaving an electrical appliance on for long periods of time may overheat it and burn it out, also threatening the whole circuit.

7   Different houses need different amounts of electricity daily, and seasonally.

8   Different houses have different types of appliances and lighting.

9   All houses have at least one appliance on through the night.

10   If an appliance is replaced, it may take a while to get used to the new model.

Now, let's look at our nervous system, that electro-chemical power which switches us on, as it corresponds to the above:

1   If brain control is not functioning properly, even healthy limbs and body may not get 'power' supplied when it is needed. Brain damage at birth or earlier, accidents, infection, tumours or shocks can cause the 'mains supply' to be disconnected, and no power to flow through to muscles and tissues.

2   If there is too high a loading on the human brain or on the nerve supply to any over-used structure or function, breakdown is inevitable. Athletes know all about this. So do weight-lifters, 'stroke' victims and those with tennis-elbow and housemaid's knees! Many occupational diseases come under this broad, general cause-factor. Although the muscles carry out the activity, the nerves send the message-orders.

The human will can be the biggest enemy of safe and comfortable nerve-loading. 'I *will* run faster'; 'I *will* paint this ceiling'; 'I *will* make a million – honestly – before I'm forty!' Many victims of multiple sclerosis lie along this road of excessive will power and insufficient nerve-strength to carry out extreme physical demands, especially the MS athletes.

Rest, cutting off the power after an overload, is essential. Your washing machine does it! Are you less aware of nature's rules?

3   So-called 'hyperactive' children or adults can burn themselves out in too high an activity of flashing electrical discharge. No electrical system is safe (to yourself or to others) when

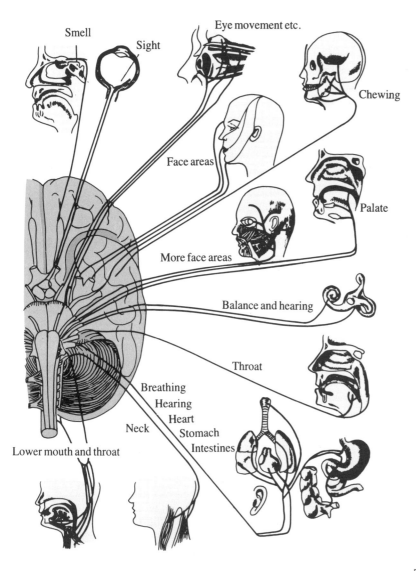

Smell

Sight

Eye movement etc.

Chewing

Face areas

Palate

More face areas

Balance and hearing

Throat

Breathing
Hearing
Heart
Stomach
Intestines

Neck

Lower mouth and throat

The human computer

constant, loud, high-voltage cracks, fizzes and sparks are not *earthed* in some way. Gardening; lying on your back on the beach or on a lawn; walking barefoot; even a massage with someone else's hands and gentle oils against your skin: all these have an *earthing* effect, taking away the high electrical discharge safely. The earth is a great producer of energy and also a great absorber of it.

4   Never expect more energy from an individual than can be safely conducted. The iris is an invaluable means of determining what type of energy is genetically available for life, and also whether this potential energy is flowing or is impeded in some correctable way. Don't ask a low-energy person to climb mountains. A 5 amp wire is unable to carry 30 amps. On the other hand, don't expect a 30 amp nervous system to need lots of rest!

5   Every nerve fibre is surrounded by insulation made of fatty material, called the myelin sheath. Some of this insulation derives from the compound cholesterol, so here's a reason why a diet low in cholesterol may not be such a good thing! Since the liver manufactures cholesterol every single day, a healthy liver is also essential for a soundly-insulated nervous system to function efficiently.

A thick, strong nerve sheath enables all sorts of nerve messages to travel along the wires together, and each message remains whole and accurate. Those of you with thinner and less well-insulated nerve fibres, may well say. 'One thing at a time is all I can handle without getting flustered and panicky, or forgetting, or getting it all wrong.' Multiple sclerosis patients are also found in this 'electrical' group, where the combination of a prolonged overload dictated to by extreme over-riding will power has broken down the myelin sheath, and the nerve messages have become fainter and weaker as the weeks and long months of overload continue.

6   Some of the damage from 5 (above) is caused by the length of time the nervous system is switched on 'high'. Even mechan-

Myelin nerve sheath

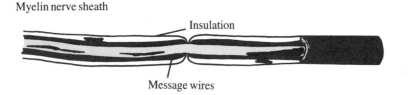

Insulation

Message wires

Every nerve fibre is surrounded by insulation made of fatty material called the myelin sheath. A thick strong nerve sheath enables all sorts of messages to travel along the wires together, each message remaining whole and accurate.

ical and electrical appliances need rest! I can remember when the first instruction from any medical doctor was: 'Go to bed and stay there until you feel better and stronger.'

Rest is such an essential part of the repair and relaxation processes after long contraction in use, that your body screams out to you when it is needed. If you ignore the signals, you're over-heating the human appliance.

Many and varied disease symptoms arise from prolonged overloads. It's common today to call the overloads 'stress'. Depending on whether the brain end or the body end is the 'over-heated' zone, you can experience almost any symptom at all, from mental irritability to nervous breakdown (at the brain end) and from ordinary fatigue to pain and limitation of use, swelling, inflammation and tissue damage.

When your body says rest, then *rest*! If you cannot, or if your head over-rides your body's plea for mercy, be aware that you've started an *illness* pattern as well as that larger bank account or whatever special goal you hope to achieve.

7   Different amounts of 'electricity' are needed for different tasks, and from year to year. There will be seasonal variation and varying demands between night and day. While we sleep, rest is supposed to recharge and restore the nervous system and the brain ready for whatever demands will be made the next day. Insomnia and poor energy go hand in hand, especially if you filled yesterday and the day before that, and even further back, with task activity.

8   While you sleep, the *active* side of your nervous system should be completely closed down. You should flop and arrange yourself in random, non-load-bearing postures. But although a lot of your electrical 'appliances' are switched off, your nervous system still keeps plugging along, mostly on what we call its *parasympathetic* track. The processes of breathing, digestion and absorption, and some fluid circulation, are still under the watchful eye of your vagus nerve, the tenth cranial nerve.

Many of the automatic processes that tick along quietly while you are asleep are inhibited if your sympathetic nervous system continues to function strongly. The opposing branches of the nervous system cannot both act at once efficiently. You can't relax muscles and contract them at the same time, and it is very hard to sleep if you are physically tense. The states of contraction and relaxation are poles apart electrically!

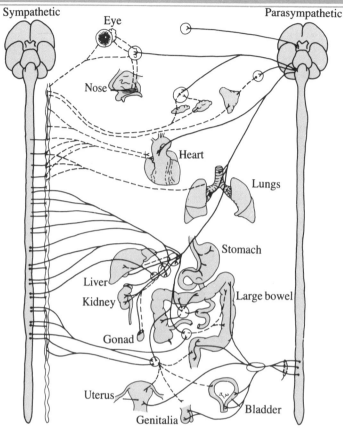

Sympathetic

Parasympathetic

Eye

Nose

Heart

Lungs

Stomach

Liver

Kidney

Large bowel

Gonad

Uterus

Bladder

Genitalia

The two halves of the nervous system

The control of household heating and cooling appliances – the refrigerator and the hot water system and the air-conditioning – is often automatic. Your body temperature, too, is automatically controlled at night. You sweat if it is too hot, move around the bed if it is too cold; and this continues even though one section of the control mechanism, your conscious control, is almost shut down. But it is still there, alerting you if a door blows open, or a child cries, or your teenagers don't arrive home when they are expected. Activity can be quickly summoned when it is necessary.

Relaxation when necessary is harder to establish. You need the *reverse* of will power, the opposite of strength, the 'letting-go' so many of those relaxation-tapes murmur about.

9   Many children who battle against sleep at bedtime need far more physical activity than they are getting. This way the sympathetic nervous system can be used and tired out, leaving the stage for the parasympathetic to dream on. Too many children sit in front of a television set for hours watching *action* movies and blood-and-thunder car chases with their adrenal glands racing and their sympathetic nervous systems highly active. No wonder they can't sleep for hours! A bedtime story told in a soft voice or soothing music may fix that bedtime battle. Give them their physical exercise straight instead of vicariously on television, and the problem won't arise. Tired little muscles will flop, and in no time they're off!

10   If part of your nervous system has been damaged, it may take much re-training; and physiotherapy, chiropractic, massage and exercise must be used to get you used to the differently function- ing section of the system and its limitations and strengths. You must slowly relearn what was once a simple reflex action. 'I have a new oven,' is the cook's best excuse for burnt scones and soggy roasts – for a while!

Specialised senses

The practical running of a human nervous system has many parallels in the communications industry. Your eyes transmit thousands of images a minute to the brain. Your ears listen to a frequency-wave-pattern and the brain calls it a motor car, or Frank Sinatra. Your taste buds react to what your thymus gland has told them in infancy is a 'good' or a 'bad' food for you. Your nose translates a chemical formula into rose or jasmine, and the smell of fresh-baked bread conveys you into the memory-teasing midst of your grandmother's kitchen.

The special senses, including that protective and defensive one of 'touch', communicate much information to you about your environment. Children, especially, use these sense organs which are really a part of the cranial nervous system, in the business of learning about life. Don't stop them educating their nervous systems by looking, touching, smelling, tasting and listening!

On the other hand, don't inhibit their natural, healthy selec- tivity of what's good and what's not good for their systems by restricting their exposure to objects of these special senses. Children banging saucepan lids together are programming their computers with sounds to which they can refer other sounds later. Feeling the dress of a lady in the supermarket queue is part of a toddler's education, not a moral lapse to be slapped out immediately. Watching the rain fill up the gutters and then overflow will teach a child more about hydraulic power than an equation on a blackboard later in life. Don't cramp this self-education by experience kind of learning.

What keeps the nervous system healthy?

A few simple nutrients determine the health and strength of the body's entire nervous system. The phosphates are right in there, with calcium phosphate, magnesium phosphate and potassium phosphate as an essential threesome. (See *The Natural Health Book*.)

Another vital element is zinc. Much has recently been written on this mineral as a cure-all for everything from epilepsy to warts! It fixes a range of seemingly diverse complaints because of its primary-site activity in the central nervous system. Silica also is vital for keeping the nerve sheath's insulation glassy-tough and resistant to wear along the fibres.

Herb teas supply essential minerals

All these minerals are best prescribed in the correct form and quantity for you by professionals, when there is therapeutic need for them in severe or prolonged illness. However, herb teas provide an easy household way of obtaining regular quantities in small amounts of all these minerals.

Valerian tea is the highest vegetable source of magnesium phosphate. Chamomile tea yields a rich quota of calcium phosphate. Either of these teas, taken at night, can increase the rest value of your sleep. Take the valerian tea slowly and carefully, though, because it can make you feel a little queasy if your liver is not a hundred per cent! Chamomile tea is a better one to start with, as it has a strong action on the vagus nerve, so relaxation can be more quickly established physically.

A third one, lettuce tea, doesn't appear much in naturopathic literature. Take a couple of the darker, outside leaves from a lettuce and wash off any garden sprays or dirt. Cover the leaves with hot water and simmer them just a minute or two. Cool and drink. The silica in lettuce is abundant, and a mild soporific effect results from a non-toxic alkaloid in the leaves. Cheap and simple!

Zinc is found in garlic and in rosehip tea. These two sources are better for daytime use!

Valerian tea is the highest vegetable source of magnesium phosphate – and it can increase the rest value of your sleep!

B-vitamins and the nervous system

A vitamin group essential to nervous system health is vitamin B complex, as those readers of *The Natural Health Book* will recall. The vitamin B group have been widely publicised as 'curing' a variety of ills resulting from many different causes. Their prime function, however, is to provide *resilience* in the nervous system. If you are bombarded by stresses, strains, and the small annoyances of everyday living, how quickly do you bounce back? How fast do you recover from a hangover or a shock, or even an illness pattern? And more to the point, how much do you laugh and sing and whistle thereafter?

If it takes you days, weeks, or even months to recover after any illness or unusual loading, check your intake of B-vitamins in the diet, and increase it by eating more seed and grain foods. If you are still below par, in spite of those actions, take a B-vitamin group supplement until you are bouncing again.

Silica and the nervous system

The silica needed for that insulation we have talked about, the nerve sheath which protects and covers the nerve fibres, is absolutely vital to the health of the nervous system. Most of the roughage areas of food, the skins, pith, coarse outside coverings of seeds and grains, even the grit with the oyster or the hooves of animals – pigsfeet are seldom on the menu now – contain silica.

But most of the silica 'impurities' have been removed from foods as they have become increasingly refined and processed, and our collective nervous-system health has declined disastrously. No wonder we need computers (with their own silicon-chips) to help our overloaded brains cope with the communications explosion technology has presented to us! Our human nervous systems, especially those of our young to teenage children, are asked to make practical sense out of a vastly more complex set of facts and figures than our immediate ancestors had to store in their brains and nervous systems. It is one of those paradoxical decisions man is faced with: the manufacture of processed food makes the money barrels roll around much more than the sale of that same food simply grown, picked and eaten in its natural state. What are we to do? Economic growth, or health – the choice is ours. In predictable fashion, man, with his ever

Bedouin women. The keen eyesight of the desert Arab is legendary, as is the resilience of his nervous system, sustained by the silica content of coarsely-ground grains, chick peas and sesame seeds!

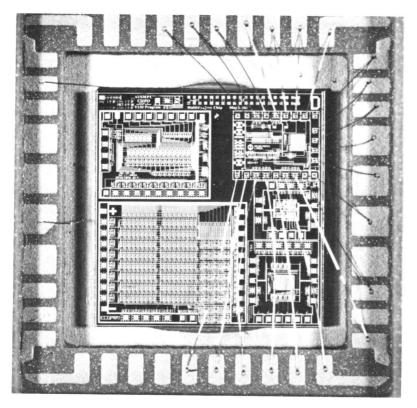

An integrated circuit board. The silicon-chip, Science's miracle of the century, has been in Nature's computer – your brain – for twenty centuries! Conduction of messages in both human and man-made computers is almost chemically identical.

more statistic-filled brain, has decided on the former.

The desert Arab who eats coarsely-ground millet and barley grains, with fresh, green or dried chick-peas, and sesame seeds in just about everything, also gains his 'peck-o'-dirt' from the desert sands blowing into his mouth and nose and onto his plate! His keen eyesight is legendary, and the resilience of his nervous system should make all we stress-ridden, civilised folk ashamed of how small, everyday loads bowl us over with nervous tension so that we need to reach for the tranquillisers!

The rougher and coarser the food we eat, the greater the silica content we gain. Unpolished grains; fibrous, raw vegetables; the skins of fruits, nuts and vegetables; silica is found in all the *unrefined* foods. Anything which needs chomping and chewing is a better source of silica than those smooth, bland, refined foods which slide down the rather more 'refined' throats of civilised populations. The collapsing nervous systems of western and 'civilised' countries need not reduce us all to decadent *ennui* and another Fall to be debated in the history books centuries hence. Silica is much more necessary for the function of our nervous systems than that better-known combination of vitamins B and C.

Marijuana

Now to a controversial but necessary policy speech. Although marijuana has been white-washed and championed, even by some of our leaders in government, the media and the professions, I must make a personal and professional statement that in my many years of consulting practice, I have come to the conclusion that it's one of the greatest threats ever to the individual nervous system.

Unlike the use of alcohol and tobacco, even unlike so-called hard drug use, the effects of marijuana show up in very definite iris symptoms. Doubling, even gaps, in and through the nerve-wreath in the iris, show that someone really is 'spaced out' when using it.

'The consensus of medical opinion is that it is not an addictive drug but there is increasing evidence that it may have long term adverse effects . . . . Recently it has been shown that the (characteristic) smell may produce the effects of cannabis smoking in an habitual smoker even when all the known active constituents have been removed.' Extract from *An Introduction to Phytopharmacy.*

Two Welsh professors of Phytopharmacy wrote this down in a standard text-book in 1975! 'No evidence against' say the champions of its use!

A recent international research organisation has now proved what iridology shows clearly: the sinapse is widened on marijuana use. In ordinary language, that means that the 'gap' between the jumping signal-transfer along *all* body nerves is greater, needing more energy to bridge it and causing a loss of quality in the signal itself. Relaxed, over-large pupils can tell the same story: a parasympathetic dominance – the so-called relaxation effect of marijuana – *continues* long after each exposure to the drug. You're relaxed, all right! You're so relaxed that even an abnormal load of stress will fail to make you fight and defend yourself and others! You've become a lotus-eater, smiling happily, no matter what!

'Great', perhaps you're saying now. 'Isn't that the idea? Shouldn't man be relaxed and happy and non-aggressive?'

Of course it would be wonderful – *if* it were real. The catch is that it's not. Your nervous system is being conned! And what is even more dangerous, marijuana smokers are quite unaware that their nervous systems have dropped down in performance, in understanding, in concentration and short-term memory, in speech co-ordination, in depth perception and even in reproductive capacity!

It's terribly obvious to someone who does not use marijuana. Trying to conduct a conversation with a marijuana user is a

> 'Although the results of this research are not yet conclusive, there is strong evidence to suggest that THC suppresses the immune system of rodents and other experimental animals, and several reports point to this possibility in man . . . In subsequent investigations Nahas demonstrated that normal lymphocytes from the blood of non-marihuana smokers, when cultured in nutrient fluid in the presence of THC, cannabadiol (CBD), or cannabinol (CBN), were seriously impaired in their capacity to undergo cellular division . . . Indeed, the finding that THC and various other cannabinoid substances strongly inhibit cellular processes was fully documented by no less than 12 medical research groups at an international conference on marihuana held in Helsinki in the summer of 1975. These researchers reported that cannabis substances strongly interfere with the synthesis of DNA, RNA and protein . . .' Extract from *Marihuana Today. A Compilation of Medical Findings for the Layman* by George K. Russell.

The new and terrible disease labelled AIDS which is baffling American medical authorities may have a simple environmental answer. Marijuana users, and their children, and their children's children, will have only about *half*, or less of, their immune-defense system operational. Instead of looking at 'gay' sex-lives, or another 'virus' as the culprit, investigate marijuana-usage as the terribly destructive agent it really is!

frustrating exercise to all! Users think they're uttering wise and gentle philosophies; all a non-user sees is someone conning their own nervous system. The slower eyelid drop in blinking; the smile when talking nonsense; both show a non-user just how much the efficiency of that nervous system has been lowered.

And the user has no idea that it is happening.

Scores of our patients complain of the following symptoms: constant tiredness; an inability to study and remember; constant and recurrent small illnesses which won't go (colds, skin blemishes, genital herpes, and Herpes simplex or 'cold sores'); lack of muscular co-ordination; and great difficulty coping with ordinary day-to-day stress unless marijuana is resorted to.

Marihuana Today* gives some frightening statistics on DNA change (your children will be human mutants whether you like it or not); and vitamin B_{12} is, of course, intrinsically partnered with DNA. Your major anti-stress vitamin, the B-group complex, is governed by the master catalyst B_{12}. Marijuana usage lowers and changes your own greatest defence against life's everyday challenges. Of course you then have to rely on it more and more! Your own defence system is being eroded. No wonder herpes gets you in its many forms, when vitamin B_{12} and your own whole DNA structure is your only defence against herpes viruses!

Without going into the above statements any further, I would, however, like to utter my own warnings in order to even up the minimal to almost non-existent arguments *against* marijuana use. I do know that if I wanted a docile, passive population who would not object, not complain and let me get away with authoritarian government, I would make sure that marijuana was freely available and its use defended! I also know that if I wanted to weaken any nation's will to defend itself against an aggressor, I would do the same!

The state of unreality in which users of marijuana live is horribly obvious to non-users. The dangers of that vague and super-relaxed driver who thinks he's driving happily and super-safely, but is a menace to other drivers and pedestrians, are only apparent to non-users! Other, marijuana-using drivers and pedestrians dwell in a land where unreality rules, too, so they see no cause for alarm.

If you wish all your body cells to be whole and function efficiently, especially if you wish to live in the real world with a strong nervous system which enjoys life and its challenges, and with a strong defence against illness (as well as threats to our human condition), perhaps you should reconsider your beliefs

*George K. Russell, *Marihuana Today*, Myrin Institute for Adult Education, New York, 1980.

Lavender oil for calming the nervous system; chamomile tea; valerian root capsules; yoga breathing; even rolled-oats porridge; all are simple and effective for your nervous system's 'off' switch – the relaxing half.

on marijuana usage. To those non-users who know what I'm talking about, stick to your guns, and live your lives with a sound nervous system, good immune responses, and a realistic view of the world: be it good or bad, at least your body has not been deluded, and your nervous system will faithfully communicate the true state of things to you.

'It's One of God's good herbs,' is how a grower described it on a television programme recently. So are Deadly Nightshade, hemlock, and foxglove! It would take a botanist who is also a homoeopath and a herbalist to explain to this gently-smiling, passive advocate of using marijuana that plants, like people, are not all good! *Cannabis indica* used medicinally in Indian culture is a very different matter from the ways in which South American strains of *Cannabis sativa* are utilised – the latter are differently prepared, contain different percentages of cannabinoids, etc., and are *habitually* taken.

For my part, I'm into silica, vitamin B, and all the other vitamin and mineral supports for my nervous system that I can get. My intelligence is not so great that I want to give some of it away!

And I'll add a caution for other non-users who want to maintain their health and their ability to defend themselves: have you considered that if the private cultivation and use of marijuana is legalised, it will be only a spaced-out step away until its use in public places is also approved? If having cigarette-smoke blown in your face infuriates you, how much worse will it be if the sickly-sweet odour of marijuana clings to the curtains and table-cloths in restaurants, and to your hair and clothing as well! Whether you like it or not, your nervous system may suffer from its effects in much the same way as non-smokers are affected by tobacco smoking, whether they want it or not!

Let's stop pretending that we 'civilised' human beings have superior brains and nervous systems! Those so-called primitive races can run rings around us, nervous systems included! And while we busily patronise them with shipments of powdered milk, white rice, infant milk formulas – even white sugar – calling it aid to underdeveloped countries, let's give some thought to the coarse whole foods, including often the skins, hair and bones, which produce the resilient nervous systems that enable them to endure the sort of hardships, challenges and deprivations that would have us queueing up to complain to the Ombudsman or scuttling home for a joint or two before bed!

The number of school children smoking marijuana would astound those teachers and parents who are non-users. After maybe ten years of habitual use (unfortunately it is becoming common in some areas for 5, 6, and 7 year olds to be found puffing homemade reefers) these teenagers may be *unemployable*, especially by employers who don't want to know about marijuana. The signs of usage are so obvious – that meaningless smile, relaxed musculature, dull, heavily-blinking eyes and slow nerve response. There is no great incentive for a prospective employer to hire such cloud-cuckoo-land youngsters! And the clincher is so horrible: they think they're bright, witty, sophisticated and capable!

We even have user-parents who offer tiny babies and toddlers a puff to help them enjoy life, too. The common characteristic of all drug users emerges on questioning: an over-violent defence, or a rather snooty condemnation of non-users as 'unenlightened'. To either of these I retort rather bluntly: 'If *my* light's out I know it; if yours is out you say it's fireworks night!' A supercilious, vacant (though meant to be enlightened) smile is the standard 'gap' response.

I would rather treat a heroin addict, an alcoholic, or try to penetrate the blank-wall, refusal-to-listen, forty-cigarettes-a-day smoker than I would a marijuana user. The first three know what they're doing to themselves: the media and health-care professionals have seen to that. But marijuana users don't know what the consequences of their habit are, because almost no public information, in the professional sense, has been made available. Most members of the media either openly defend it, or say 'not proven' after an investigation of the adverse effects.

Let's hear from some of you now! There *is* a large body of evidence about marijuana's adverse effects on health and the social and economic aspects of our society. 'Dope' it used to be called! Need I say more? 'Stoned' is, perhaps, an even better adjective to describe its effects. If you had been hit on the head by rocks and were suffering from concussion, your nervous system would be in approximately the same condition!

Let's stop talking about that currently fashionable illness, stress, and call it by its true name: loading, challenge, job, work, decisions, worries, fears – take your pick. There is no disease called stress, only far too many nervous systems that can't stand up to life. Strengthen *yours* the way nature has always provided.

5 *To Breathe or not to Breathe? the Respiratory System*

Is breathing a fundamental and built-in ability, or must human babies learn it like any other skill? Obstetrician's handbooks often mention the 'hang-'em-up-by-the-heels and slap-'em immediately after birth' routine as the way to 'a good deep breath to get the lungs to expand fully'. But what about the exhalation to follow? Does the newborn, blinking under those blinding hospital lights and surrounded by rushing forms and voices, fill the lungs, only to find out by a process of cyanosing panic that they must also be *emptied* before the next oxygen-laden breath can follow? As every asthma sufferer can tell you, it is easy to breathe in; the hard part is breathing *out*. So there's your first-born, dangling head-down in mid-air, panicking!

Is it any wonder that such an incredible experience as this first taste of life out of the uterus's cushioning amniotic fluid, has produced the asthma generation? Every difficult asthmatic exhalation is a repetition of that first experience: panic, as a result of oxygen deprivation.

The same condition kills hundreds in theatre fires, night-club blazes and hotel disasters – panic caused by an inability to breathe. Exhalation becomes impossible and, in any case, oxygen is lost in the combustion. Not that there is anything in fire itself to produce panic; panic occurs when the diaphragm tightens, the chest muscles contract, the lungs lose efficiency and all that is left to breathe is carbon dioxide waste products, not oxygen.

Contrast this with the simple experience of natural childbirth, which is not new to even the most 'backward' primitive tribes, but is comparatively new to us as it is re-discovered by our so-called civilised, over-medicated, developed cultures. Not only is birth generally simple and satisfying for the mother, but one important difference changes the child's first experience of the world outside the uterus. The newborn is allowed to crawl gently upwards to the mother's breast (just as many animal young do instinctively), before the umbilical cord is cut.

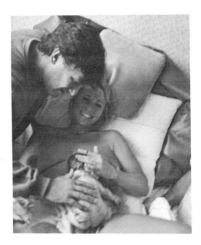

The first harsh experience of air! Newborn is allowed to crawl gently upwards to the mother's breast *before* the umbilical cord is cut.

This process may take a good half-hour, mother massaging her baby's body gently all the way, and oxygen still available from her via the placenta and umbilical cord. The child breathes easily and safely, still on the same pulse as the mother and synchronising with her breathing, until the experience of *air* instead of fluid, is safely gained. Placental blood supply to the child gradually lessens. At this point the umbilical cord empties of blood, so there is no need even to tie it off after it is severed. The child has learned gently what will be perhaps the most important lesson for its health through life: the art of gaining oxygen in sufficient quantity not only to maintain breathing efficiency, but so that this oxygen can be used in one of its most unsung roles, as a disease-fighter.

Have you ever wondered why TB sufferers are sent to sanatoriums in the high mountains to recover? Because those scarred lungs need to learn to breathe again. Lungs have to work harder at higher altitudes, and although part of the treatment also meant that the patients escaped the smog caused by coal fires in the cities (and nowadays the chemical smogs) increased efficiency in breathing was the aim.

Asthma = panic!

If the Asthma Foundation talks to the pediatricians, perhaps mutual understanding will protect our most vulnerable citizens, the new-born, from a future involving those frightful regimes of puffers, inhalers, humidifiers, steroids and panic, the lifelong fate of a humiliating number of people in our so-called 'enlightened' age. We can be really very dumb in many instances where animals and primitive cultures evolved past us centuries ago!

Of course, I can hear you saying to yourself, 'What about the air pollution now? Isn't that the reason for an increase in asthma figures, especially in the very young?' Perhaps – but we all breathe the same air, don't we? The difference is that if you were lucky enough to be born quietly at home some fifty or sixty years ago (or even in recent years with a natural birth) you breathe the same air but you don't suddenly acquire *asthma* (or panic). You may suffer from catarrh or nasal sensitivity, even red eyes, but you don't react to poor oxygen availability with panic/asthma. The disease should be called this, because the two words describe the same physiological experience.

So what's the next step, if you have already learned the panic/asthma experience and call yourself an asthmatic? The newest treatment methods involve expensive and prolonged re-education in relaxation classes which teach you: 'Don't panic, don't panic, and you won't have an attack of asthma'! This new medical break-through is just too much for my common horse-sense to applaud, I'm sorry to say.

For those of us who still breathe the apology for air we're doomed to put up with in cities, and increasingly in the countryside as industry is decentralised, there is a way our gasps for oxygen can be made much more positive. Did you know that one of the jobs of vitamins is to *reduce* the body's need for oxygen by increasing the blood's efficiency at moving oxygen around the body? What this means is that you can fare better with less.

Our ancestors had the best of both conditions: cleaner air, and diets containing more foods much higher in vitamin E than ours are now. Replace this lost ease of breathing by taking vitamin E supplements if your stubborn belief that all carbohydrates are fattening, and cholesterol is bad for your heart, keeps you away from foods very high in vitamin E such as oats, buckwheat, wheat (especially the wheat germ), egg yolks, etc. We will look more closely at the cholesterol myth later; for the moment, breathing is the important issue, not a paper-thin silhouette and no energy!

Oxygen: the purifying power

Now let's look at oxygen in another role: its ability to fight disease. Yet another medical breakthrough recently took my breath away, if you'll pardon the pun! 'Oxygen may have a role to play in the prevention of tumours, cancers and all types of growths and malignancies', I read in a technical report from another one of those billion-dollar Foundations. The essence of the report was that the better your oxygen-carrying ability is, the less likely you are to develop cancer.

So what's new? It's been a naturopathic precept since Imhotep! Oxygen causes 'burning', that is it aids the combustion of rubbish in bodies, just as it makes fire possible in air. As any fireman could tell you, if you remove air with its oxygen, fire cannot burn. Chemists and physicists and explosives scientists know all about that. If the blood stream lacks oxygen, all sorts of waste products remain 'unburned' by the iron 'fire' which normally consumes them in the bloodstream and elsewhere and eliminates them through the bowels. 'Dirty blood' may once again be the useful classification for cancer that it used to be, once science 'proves' again that unburned, unexcreted residues of certain kinds provide ideal feeding grounds for the nourishment of abnormal cells and random cells.

Recently I heard one Australian medical team report that 'Cancer is not a disease, but a long degenerative process. Symptoms only appear in the final stages: the process may start twenty-five years earlier, or even from the cradle.' How right these few enlightened medical researchers are! Dr Wilhelm Reich, early this century, called it the 'cancer biopathy'. One of the predisposing conditions he looked for was poor breathing and therefore lack of that vital energy, oxygen molecules. His books were burned, his students harassed for his medical 'heresy', and he died in gaol in America. How this gentle and concerned man must be grinning wryly somewhere now!

While patterns of breathing difficulty may stem from an experience during the first few minutes of life, the resulting poor oxygenation may last a lifetime. Secondary infection has a far easier pathway if lungs are less than efficient with every breath. It is harder to stay healthy and fight off infection if oxygen is in short supply, for iron becomes less effective at burning off body wastes each day. The body then harbours the remains of dead bacteria, cells which have become viral-hosting, and excess mucus produced as a defence against the irritants and pollutants in the air which inflame and weaken the mucus linings of nose, throat, bronchial tree and lungs.

The lungs and waste-disposal

Did you know that the lungs are the major agent of elimination, not only of carbon dioxide as the waste product of breathing, but of carbonic acid wastes which accumulate in tissues throughout the body as metabolic remains after nervous system usage? If you have played a gruelling game of football, enjoyed a hard day's sailing, a weekend's skiing, or even a walk round the block at lunchtime, you have begun to move those tissue wastes towards the organs of excretion. The lungs are one of a committee of four which handles waste disposal: bowels, kidneys, skin and lungs. If the lungs are efficient and carbon dioxide is well removed, the load on the other three organs is correspondingly lighter.

Many of the degenerative processes of major illness begin because the organs of excretion cannot get rid of waste products as fast as they build up. You can improve your chances of good health by exercise, for this *always* increases excretion. Now do you understand why you puff and pant during exercise? The lungs/ bellows are only one part of you which benefits as their functional loading is stepped up; pulmonary arteries work harder and better oxygenated blood – 'cleaner' blood – is given to the heart to work with.

Many different herbs are used for treating the various parts of the respiratory process. Elecampagne stimulates lung linings, helping them expel more carbon dioxide – pumping it out – by a physiological improvement in the pumping of gases. Coltsfoot loosens congealed old waste products (tars deposited from tobacco smoking, air pollutant wastes, residual puddles of infection from old bronchitis attacks, pneumonias, etc.).

Grindelia relaxes the hair-like cilia which line the bronchial passages, for these become clogged and sticky when excess mucus is produced in response to the penetration of the body space through mouth and nose by infective and irritant materials.

Stinging nettle, that common weed despised as a pest and

Ocean sailors have the best of both aids to breathing – cleaner air and hard physical exercise. If a day's sailing leaves you exhilarated and naturally ready for a good night's sleep, it also leaves you healthier, with body wastes oxygenated away.

Euphorbia hirta can lessen many folk's hypersensitivity to flower pollen, grass seed, cigarette smoke and so on.

nuisance in the garden, is a powerful arterial blood tonic and improver of the oxygen-carrying ability of the bloodstream.

Euphorbia hirta, a plant which grows in Australia, can lessen the hypersensitivity of many folk whose mucus linings are trigger-happy when they encounter flower pollens, grass seeds, cigarette smoke, cold draughts and heated rooms.

And so the list goes on. We can add garlic to it to help fight off new infection while we're getting rid of past damage; cod liver oil can boost A and D vitamins to strengthen mucus linings all through the body.

Don't be tempted, though, to self medicate on all the above in a burst of enthusiastic resolve to clean up your 'chubes'! Remember the principles of naturopathy: the size of the dose of any medication will determine whether it's beneficial or harmful to each individual.

Consult your professional naturopath or health adviser initially to find out what *you* require, in what quantity and why. Then you can go away and do it all much more accurately, safely and effectively.

Are you beginning to grasp how *simple* good health can be? In the light of the intellectual advances of the past few centuries, we often ignore our older knowledge gained from accumulated experiences over tens of thousands of years of the world around us. Today, however, if we wish to know *why* certain herbs have successfully rid our respiratory systems of disease for so long, we have analyses of their chemical contents available. We can now 'prove' (if science demands we keep proving the obvious!) why these herbs act as they do.

No matter what 'disease' affects respiration, these herbs work against it! Emphysema, tuberculosis, cystic fibrosis, asthma, allergic bronchitis, a chest cold, a persistent cough, the 'flu', silicosis – *all* will begin to improve, in varying degrees and at varying speeds, once they are treated in different dosages and combinations which contain in highly complex chemical partnerships the ingredients needed to improve respiratory efficiency. That's how the word 'nature' came to be applied to naturopathic treatments. Give all the various parts of you the right ingredients to function with, and you can't help but be healthy. Herbs are ideal – easily absorbed and compatible with your body fluids so that your body can be re-arranged chemically and become more efficient at living.

What's the difference between a herbal treatment for disease and dietary re-arrangement? Not much! The time factor will probably make the greatest difference; one can eat stinging nettles as a green vegetable (they taste like excellent spinach) take nettle tea or – even quicker – take a medicinal mixture containing nettle tincture or extract. Where a 'food' becomes a 'medicine' is a nebulous point of dosage level as well as improvement speed.

Can you see another principle of naturopathy appearing? The earlier you treat the small ups and downs of daily living and its sins of omission and commission, the less likely are you *ever* to deteriorate in time into the chronic establishment of disease. Time and quantity (measurement of what each individual needs to correct small inefficiencies as they occur) apply as much to your cold in the chest as they do to the stars on their courses!

To smoke or not to smoke?

There is enough information around for all of us now to see the path ahead of us if we smoke. If we know and can predict the eventual disease processes, why do so many of us decide to continue?

Man's arrogance can be quite amazing under scrutiny. 'It might happen to everyone else, but not to *me*,' is an attitude common to many. Graphic medical histories of deformed babies; thrombosis amputations; pictures from the morgue and forensic medicine books showing coal black streaks through tar-saturated lungs; what more does it take to convince everyone?

Tobacco smoking is what we are talking about. Marijuana-smokers have a different problem to worry about; they have such a *relaxed* respiratory system that the muscular apparatus connected with breathing loses all its oomph. One of the reasons they feel 'relaxed' (drugged would be a more appropriate word) and sleep better is because they are starved of oxygen with every puff, becoming more and more saturated with carbon dioxide.

The breathing zones of habitual marijuana smokers show *more* damage eventually than those of heavy tobacco smokers! Nowhere near enough physical or mechanical stimulus can be applied by the lungs and the bronchial tree, so not only is there less oxygen taken in for use and distribution throughout the body, but concentration, thinking ability, short-term memory and co-ordination of words and ideas is lost. Relaxed? 'Doped' would be a better description. You certainly suffer from oxygen deprivation when smoking marijuana!

Increase in deaths

Thirty years ago lung cancer was a rare disease. Today it causes more deaths in Australian men than any other cancer. Just on 3,500 men and over 600 women die each year in Australia from lung cancer. The increasing death rates have closely paralleled the increasing consumption of cigarettes. While improving diagnosis accounts for some of the rise, the experts have no doubt that a true increase in lung cancer has occurred with cigarette smoking as its cause. Similar increases have been reported world wide.

Smoking and Lung Cancer

The scientific data now clearly show that cigarette smoking is the major cause of lung cancer. Suspicion was initially aroused by the observation that most lung cancer patients were heavy cigarette smokers. Numerous statistical studies since 1931 have borne this out and have shown that the risk of lung cancer increases with the duration of smoking and the number of cigarettes smoked each day. The good news is that it decreases when a person stops smoking.

Extract from pamphlet on lung cancer published by the Anti-Cancer Council of Victoria

Is all smoking harmful?

Many patients have told me: 'I just enjoy the mechanics of smoking.' 'I like to hold something in my hands when I'm socialising.' The last is a human's way of saying 'I don't feel confident enough in this situation to be myself honestly and openly. I must be my socially-edited self, and be pleasant and charming.' (See *Iridology*, p. 179.)

As always, there is a middle way. Many herbal smoking mixtures can be made at home from simple aromatic plants, spices and oils.

Coltsfoot, mentioned above as a tonic expectorant and greatly beneficial (even as a 'smoke' inhalation) to lungs and bronchial tree, is often used as the basis for such mixtures; dried lavender; dried rosemary; peppermint and other mints; cloves and cinnamon; patchouli oil or rose oil or your own specially favourite oil can be added.

If you like smoking, but dislike the damaging effects of those two plants, marijuana and tobacco, there are a thousand others to choose from. (Leaving smoking as the domain of two plants only is just as self-limiting as is our usual beverage choice of 'tea or coffee'. When one considers how many thousands of plants can be made into herbal teas using the leaves, flowers, berries and even roots, and the beneficial effects they will have on various body organs and functions, it seems foolish to limit our warm drinks to two only!)

Ask your herbal 'chemist' or health store for do-it-yourself books if you wish to make your own combinations of herbal smoking mixtures, or enquire about ready-made herbal cigarettes, which are often available. One of the first effects you'll notice from them is a loosening and coughing up of unbelievable amounts of rubbish which may have been impeding your oxygen intake and usage for years! It's 'all in the cause of economy' as the song goes; economy of effort and energy needed to maintain good health.

The value of aromatic oils

As well as those plants I have mentioned, there are many others which can improve breathing efficiency. The inhalation of aromatic oils can accomplish marvels very pleasantly. Penetrating oils rubbed on the chest are similarly effective.

Read up on these home methods of loosening and removing the residues and waste products of breathing in the many good herbal books now available – preferably those written by practising herbalists and naturopaths. Some other books are fantastically 'magical' and 'olde worlde', and beautifully illustrated, but they can be sources of information three or four times removed from accuracy.

Look for books containing *practical* instructions on how to do it all, not those offering lose advice like 'comfrey has been used to treat bronchitis', but with no further instructions as to whether you rub it on, drink it down, eat it fresh or steamed, or dance around it at midnight!

So take a few deep breaths! Surely, you may say, all the long

A few drops of peppermint oil, a small basin of boiling water, and a towel to put over the head. Too expensive? Too difficult? No, too *simple* for those clever scientific folk to believe in its safety and its efficacy. And there's no need for the complicated 'tent' effect this nineteenth-century gentleman has constructed!

lists of medically-named diseases affecting the lungs cannot be treated with a handful of plants, foods, teas and oils? Why not? Is it an insult to your intelligence, acquired painfully during the process called your education, or is it going to be a compliment to your wisdom, handed to you in cell-memory for thousands of years, that you see the *simplicity* of it all? Different doses are certainly required, and at different strengths for different periods of time, so *all* your intelligence will not be wasted, but life *was* meant to be easy – not easy as in lazy but easy as in simple.

Treating causes, not symptoms, of disease

A chiropractor may do a series of simple dorsal spine adjustments of D3 or D4 and remove your asthma. Acupuncturists trained in the classical schools will do a series of treatments where needles may go in everywhere *except* around the 'sick' respiratory areas. Homoeopaths may look at your ancestor's death from tuberculosis and whether your symptoms are worse before midday, in coming to a decision that one single plant, in high potency and tiny concentration is your treatment.

In any modality, it is comparatively simple to remove the symptoms of disease; it is much harder to remove the *causes*. Your dorsal spine, weakened by bad posture for years, may slip back to its former state after a while, and then you will need another series of visits to your chiropractor, or acupuncturist, or whoever. Naturopaths, especially present-day ones (who after much experience are beginning to get a faint glimmer of the *real* causes of 'disease') are going a step further and looking to eradicate the cause-factors so that 'disease' as formerly experienced *cannot* happen again.

To take a medical example: cortizone ointments of various kinds are used to 'remove' such named diseases as eczema, psoriasis, and so on. In fact, the symptoms are suppressed only, the cause-factors remain. Likewise, Ventolin will ease your breathing but not stop you getting further asthma attacks. An old-fashioned herbalist will give you a bottle of bronchitis-mixture each winter when your bronchitis returns – same principle.

The new breed of naturopath, however, wrestles with a far greater problem, digging, delving, questioning, observing, relating and never stopping until some real underlying cause is found.

This is what the iris of the eye records, not the medically-named

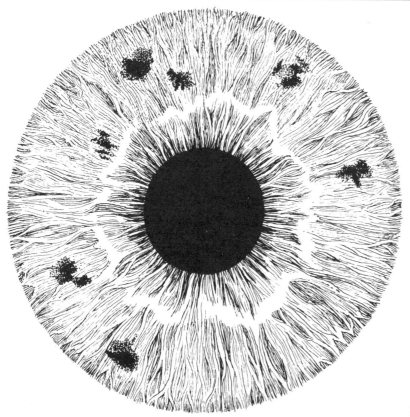

Psoric spots are special signs in the iris – any zone under a psoric spot *can* produce out-of-balance reactions some or all of the time.

A simple magnifying torch is the inexpensive tool needed by an iridologist. If a photographic record is to be made of the patient's iris, a much more sophisticated camera set-up is required.

disease in perhaps the chest zone or respiratory zones of the iris where science says it *should* be (or else all Iridology is rubbish) but perhaps in the liver zone (a difficulty with vitamins A and D and therefore a mucus lining sensitivity in the respiratory organs which is greater than it needs to be). Or it could even be in the 'anxiety' zone in the iris (the different degrees of fear, panic and apprehension which many newborn encounter as the first of life's experiences). Nothing may show in the respiratory zones at all!

This evolution of medicine called the 'new naturopathy' will treat such a patient for the disease of fear or of vitamin deficiency rather than a blanket ailment called bronchitis. Causes can now be found and treated, rather than symptoms being placated, soothed, buried or even removed by surgery. How much defeat can scientific medicine accept when the best of its new developments is to remove large sections of small intestine surgically, so that the too great a quantity of the wrong kind of food the patient still wants to eat, because of emotional deprivation which causes the craving, cannot be absorbed as much in the shorter length of intestine?

Cutting the baby's head off because it's crying could be the next 'breakthrough'! It is time for a rational look at the causes of disease, the *real* reasons, not an increasingly expensive, intrusive and desperate hacking away of symptoms as fast as they occur. There is no reason for symptoms to occur if their causes are removed.

So how's all that philosophy affecting your breathing? Do you now know a little more about some of the reasons for respiratory 'disease'? Did it explain some of the *real* causes of your last asthma attack, or the bronchitis you get every winter because you can't be bothered wearing an overcoat and you don't like the smell of garlic or the taste of cod liver oil? You are halfway to being what all of us can be, our own physician, if you have been a respiratory patient for years, *but* you've begun attending relaxation classes and saying 'no' to milkshakes and 'yes' to Indian curries loaded with fenugreek which makes you sneeze and cough and blow and feel great afterwards.

Natural remedies for the respiratory tract

Those vitamins A and D are also strongly supportive in strengthening and de-sensitising the mucus linings of nose, throat, bronchial tree and lungs. That dreaded green-glass bottle full of white oily glug called cod liver oil emulsion was a daily after-breakfast ordeal for many children several generations ago; hardly any of them were asthmatic, though, nor did they become so!

The fishy taste of the pure oil is now disguised in gelatine capsules and is far easier to take, even for the smallest members of the family. Fenugreek as a tea, as sprouts, or even in curry spices, makes its own D_2 and D_3 form of the vitamin and also contains vitamin A. So do nettles and kelp. Include some of these simple food and drink sources of the A and D vitamins as everyday items in your diet if you have a family tree which displays breathing difficulties.

Another standby for those folk with 'sensitive' respiratory tracts is horseradish. Two of my previous books* mention its use in more detail. Keep it on the table as a condiment/dressing if pollens and grasses make you sneeze and sniffle, and the first cold air to hit you on late winter afternoons or early winter mornings fills your nose and throat wetly with mucus. Such over-active mucus linings can produce the social disease of tissues and 'a-tishoos'! Sneezing, throat-clearing and nasally-

The Natural Health Book; The Natural Health Cookbook

clogged speech can ruin your social ratings and send you running from a room at the wrong moment altogether! Horseradish does help. If you use it regularly as a condiment, the likelihood of having to take it therapeutically in tablet form at some stage is lessened.

The upper part of the respiratory tract (the antrums and upper sinus zones) is easier to treat for respiratory problems than the lower zone. Gravity works for you when you sneeze and blow, but gravity works *against* you when you have to cough or exhale waste products from the lungs, the lower respiratory spaces.

Let aromatic oils do much of the hard, but very pleasant-smelling, work of loosening, soothing and de-sensitising those upper sinuses. Peppermint oil inhalations are surprisingly breath-taking in strength, and powerful looseners! Thymol in peppermint is also antiseptic, so you can really slaughter those bacteria and viruses. Just add a few drops of the oil to a bowl of boiling water; drape a towel over your head and around the basinful of strong minty fumes, and inhale for five minutes. 'Post-nasal drip' people will find this simple treatment quite miraculous!

Another standby for the 'sensitive' respiratory tract folk is horseradish.

Another aromatic oil useful for treating those upper respiratory tract zones is aniseed. Buy a small bottle of this from your health store or herbal chemist and it will last you for many months, even years. Just place your finger over the bottle's neck, tip it up gently, then touch the back of your tongue with the aniseed-oiled finger – just a drop. Anethol, its most powerful aromatic component, will deaden the taste-buds and tongue surface for a few seconds, and then the aromatic oil will penetrate upwards into the deep bone cavities of sinuses, shaking loose old congealed mucus and even old dried blood from earlier sinus infections. It will gently soothe any dry-bone areas where repeated infection or surgical scraping has almost destroyed linings. Simple? Not too simple, I hope, for you to try it.

Manufacturers spend millions of dollars improving efficiency of product use; technologists invent machines and gadgets of increasing efficiency for use; vehicles become splendidly co-ordinated, smoothly-functioning models of efficient fuel consumption. What about us? Are you content to spend your life breathing inefficiently? Try some up-and-down, in-and-out air with the simple supports I mentioned to aid you, and experience *efficient* oxygenation. Your quality of life — and your life span — should show obvious benefits.

6 Let's Hear it for the Heart and the Blood, the Fluids, and the Lymph Chain

THE heart is the last-ditch organ when body loads become too great to carry. With no partner-organ to turn to – unlike other organs in the body – there is no off-load mechanism to relieve it and give it a rest; it works around the same average rate and volume every minute of every day of your life. If it is actually attacked, as in rheumatic fever or an angina pectoris 'squeeze', it can quickly enlarge itself, even double or treble its rate or pumping-volume to meet the emergency, but it can't appeal for help to any other organ in the body. Of course, it has to be the greatest death-producer!

But 'avoiding heart disease', the subject of many leaflets, articles and foundation grants, can have you believing that all you need to do to keep your heart going for a much longer, healthier life-span, is stop eating cholesterol-rich foods and animal fats, and walk to work each day. Certainly that all helps greatly, but if kidneys are labouring badly, adrenalin levels are too high (or too low), your thyroid is lazy or abnormally racing, your blood pressure is constantly over-high or – even more insidiously dangerous – too low, in other parts of the body (carotid and other cerebral arteries, renal arteries, portal vein etc.) it's the heart which must take these other loading factors as well as its own.

So there's your heart, never taking a 'sickie' or a day off; working for three score years and ten at a maintenance-free rate which no machine could duplicate. What *is* the best way to help it?

Beware of sudden shocks!

Hearts can take an incredible load if it is applied gradually. The problems begin (and often 'end' someone!) when too sudden an increase in load is applied. Every sportsman in training knows that increasing effort-goals can be safe; indeed, it can even be good for the health and fitness of the whole body. But in super-vised training, no load is applied until the athlete shows he or she is ready for it by demonstrating an ability to cope successfully and safely with the present load.

Away from the sporting scene, too many of us in ordinary life are suddenly asked to carry loads without any previous condi-tioning or warning. A loved one dies suddenly; a car crashes; the house catches fire; you're knocked down in unexpected physical violence; your perfectly friendly overture is rebuffed with shouted verbal violence: on it could go, shock after shock. Surgery can impose its own shock when pain and trauma follow anaesthesia and its consequent depletion of adrenalin. 'Surgical shock' vic-tims die not from the surgery, but from the sudden shock the heart receives.

There's certainly no way that we can be forewarned about these deals from Dame Fortune, but there is a homoeopathic remedy, Arnica 30X, and Bach Remedy herbal agents which can very quickly minimise the *effect* of any shock on the heart. These two remedies are all I carry with me for any emergency, physical or mental.

The heart not only takes the full brunt of any shock; it also stores the experience of shock unless these release agents are used. Many people's irises show the shadowy signs around the heart-zone of old shock experiences never really removed. The

Hearts can take an incredible load if it is applied gradually, but – too sudden an increase caused, perhaps, by unexpected physical or verbal violence can give you a jolt!

danger lies in the *next* shock they suffer, for the first and the second will be felt together, and if a third is experienced, the heart may stop altogether, under the burden of all three. A 'broken heart' can be an all-too-real cause of death!

The 'died-in-his-sleep' heart ending is the opposite of shock being the reason for death. In this case, the blood pressure may be far too low at rest, although it *may* be within low to normal range during exercise or activity. Many of the silk-type iris folk keep themselves efficiently and enthusiastically alive long past their three-score and ten years by this 'resting' of the heart as blood pressure drops way down after the quite long and heavy activity which can mark their early rising day. But if they become permanently *sedentary*, through the limitation of illness or circumstances, that resulting low blood pressure can be insufficient to keep their heart pumping strongly enough, and failing pressure, poor oxygen transport and insufficient venous return can slow the heart right down to a 'stop'.

The answer lies, as it does with all of nature, in achieving a balance between gradual loading and rest. Too much suddenly applied 'load on the back', physical or emotional, is just as bad as too little. Those enthusiastic newly-converted folk who leap out of a warm bed into a track-suit to jog three kilometres uphill may (and too often do), overload the heart drastically. Some have dropped dead before turning the last corner near their front gate. Do all your body changes, dietary re-arrangement, exercise and therapies gradually, re-training your body in slower steps rather than sudden shock-producing leaps.

Exercise is important

So far, it may look as if shock and too-sudden exercise are the main trauma hearts have to beat! But what about physical loadings like narrowing and hardening arteries, fatty yellow cholesterol clogging, and heavy fatty tissue saturation around the outside of the heart?

The answers should be getting more obvious by now. If you avoid or remove heavy shock and trauma and take moderate physical exercise at work and at play, the above problems need not arise! If you have done all the *wrong* things, however, and developed one or all of the lazy, 'fatty' heart symptoms, the best and fastest way out is still to burn up the excess fats and oils stored in your body by exercise. It is no use trying yet another diet promising you slim, trim, terrific energy, if you do nothing energetic afterwards. Any diet which has been well thought out and to which you adhere strictly can help you lose a kilo or two, but to keep yourself slimmer and less fat-saturated you must exercise.

Begin your plan by walking. Are fares on public transport so cheap that you're tempted not to? I doubt it! You'll spend more time sitting in medical waiting-rooms, sick at home in bed or even in hospital, than you'll lose by walking somewhere instead of driving.

Europeans and the English walk a lot. The dog needs its twice-daily airing winter and summer, and even if the English beer puts on a few calories, the customers walk, not drive, to and from the pub. It is a common sight to see the Italians, the Germans, the Austrians, the French and the British walking after dinner at night. Sleep comes more readily and digestion improves with a one two, one two, round the block, in the park or on a waterfront pathway. What do *you* do after dinner?

I had a satisfying conversation with a highly-respected medical man last year. We were both guests on one of those lovely summer glides around Sydney harbour on a private cruiser. As medical folk are wont to do, we gravitated towards talking 'shop'. He had recently returned from China where he had witnessed the unwrapping of a royal Chinese mummy thousands of years old. The degrees of arteriosclerosis, atherosclerosis and atheroma were found to be equal to, if not greater than, our present-day levels.

In commonsense naturopathic words, the royal princess had died with narrowed arteries inflexibly calcified, and fatty degeneration of heart and major blood vessels. Was she, too, a victim of stress, this so-called newfangled, cover-all 'disease' (which is older than Methuselah!) or was it just co-incidental that she was almost certainly sedentary and never needed to lift a finger in physical activity? Was it also co-incidental that at that period of Chinese history, beet sugar was first introduced into the diet of the wealthy and the nobles? With this combination of sugar and no exercise, *any* fats eaten will be retained dangerously in the circulation. The prized dishes of fatty duck and grease-laden goose would be the last loads the comparatively young princess could not get her heart to carry.

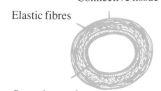

Connective tissue
Elastic fibres
Smooth muscle

The cross section of a healthy artery; when fatty substances are deposited in the inner layers, the opening in the artery narrows. High sugar intake and no exercise will be too great a load for your heart!

Cholesterol and the liver

This same medical man had come to the conclusion my patients had also taught me over many years in practice: it has nothing to do with 'stress' or cholesterol and triglyceride levels; but it has everything to do with the rate at which your liver makes cholesterol (as it does every day of your life quite normally as part of its body tasks) and the rate at which you *use* this fatty substance, and dietary fats, in activity.

In a previous book, *The Natural Health Book*, the 'Strange Case of the Irish Twins' was explored. Perhaps you should give up your struggles with calorie-counters, diet miseries and restrictions that leave you with malnutrition, at best, and anorexia nervosa at worst, and, move yourself around more!

If years of take-away foods, daily car rides to and from the station, and television immobilising you for hours every evening, have already taken their toll of your arteries, veins and heart, there are a few unbelievably simple ways of beginning to undo the damage. Do you like onions, shallots, chives, spring onions, leeks and, best of all, garlic? Go for your life to the onion family, for its members naturally control the cholesterol your liver makes each day. Have you ever wondered why so many recipes in so many cultures begin with 'crush two or three cloves of garlic'? 'Take one or two large onions,' says another. 'Sprinkle chopped chives over all,' finishes a third. It's not just to enhance the taste; it's a positive health benefit.

If the onion family give you nausea and wind, even pain, you should then be aware that your liver and its production of cholesterol may not be healthy for you. But your herbal and naturopathic way out may be to regulate your liver, not to stop eating onions!

Almost all the treatments we prescribe at the clinic for obesity begin by regulating the liver. A later chapter explains further its role in metabolism, but remember that alcohol, cigarettes and coffee, not to mention addictive drugs and pharmaceutical drug residues, inhibit the efficient function of the liver. You would be better advised to give up smoking and cut out or down on your alcohol intake and the pills you pop, rather than remove potentially good foods (as well as bad) from your diet in the mistaken belief that this is all you have to do to lose weight.

Seek professional advice

We see some disastrously unbalanced metabolisms in patients who have undertaken rigidly controlled or self-inflicted dietary change. Get professional advice *first*, from naturopath, biochemist, nutritionist or whoever else is able to extract your *individual* needs from the maze of conflicting information in the popular press and highly advertised (and costly!) products. Remember the naturopathic philosophy I discussed at the beginning of this book: you are quite different from everyone else, and so is *your* heart, *your* circulation and *your* health.

Hypertension

Hypertension has become another catch-word. Does it mean high blood pressure, or what? In its strict original meaning, it describes the over-tight contraction of muscle structures all around the body which do not relax when the task is done, but maintain a higher than comfortable pressure on both small and large blood vessels. The heart, as a large piece of smooth muscle, also feels this 'pressure' and its arteries continue to pump harder. So when your muscles are supposed to be in a relaxed state after the completion of a task, they remain contracted.

For many sufferers from hypertension sleep does not restore energy, as tense contraction is maintained until they wake up, and the time spent in bed is equivalent to running around the block all night! Sitting in a comfortable chair isn't relaxing for them, either; their hands grip the chair's arms, their neck is rigidly pulled tight into shoulders and back; thigh muscles are clamped and feet become numb and tingling; even at rest their bodies are 'uptight'.

The causes of hypertension are basic: the adrenalin which pours into the bloodstream in answer to physical or emotional overloads is not being balanced by noradrenalin, the relaxing hormone, after the time of loading has passed. After it's all over, you are still tense when you are supposed to be relaxing.

This is why Valium, one of the most widely-dispensed drugs in the western world, and marijuana, now rapidly overhauling it in popularity, appear to reduce stress. Neither of them improve your circumstances; both of them dull your consciousness of being 'uptight', that's all.

Unfortunately, while they seem to be improving your ability to relax, they are also removing much of the short-term (and long-term) ability of those muscle structures to contract again when fresh physical or mental demands occur. You have not only provided a substitute for noradrenalin, using quite different body systems, but you've tipped the scales towards manufacturing progressively *less* adrenalin, even when it's desperately needed for working without rapidly tiring, for long periods of concentration, or even for defending yourself against attack.

If you examine nature, you will find it doesn't consist of sweetness, light and non-aggression. When your comfort or your life is threatened, adrenalin pours out to give you enough 'oomph' to survive. If adrenalin is *not* available under extreme conditions, you will smile and relax while you are clobbered to death!

I feel rather responsible for a patient of mine who read my first two books, sold up his professional design practice, and began to build his own house in the bush from local stone, grow his own food, and become self-sufficient. For the first few years he was lonely, exhausted but doggedly determined to do it all. Several years more and it was done, single-handed, a magnificent, beautifully decorated castle in the bush. Friends flocked in then (whose help he could have used earlier!), and he now leads a full and happy existence.

Only he knows how much adrenalin he poured into his bloodstream for years, and the noradrenalin that flooded in to balance it when he flopped to sleep, satisfied and naturally tired out at sundown.

On his last visit to the clinic for treatment for minor strain to his back, he looked marvellous. His face glowed, his blood pressure was that of a five-year-old (he's fifty-five) and his calmness, pride and satisfaction is very apparent.

He looked at me with a twinkle. 'You know', he said, cocking his head on one side, 'I used to think it would be wonderful, out there with Mother Nature being gentle and kind and doing it all for me. I've really learned about nature; it's *warfare*! The currawongs dive-bomb the wrens who have just attacked the aphids on the cabbages the possums flattened last night. The rain washes my newly-cemented garden walls clean of three days' work. The sun scorches my plums just as the first crop is ripening. The wind blows the sheets of corrugated iron off the roof before I can nail them all down. And you know what? I've learned how to win every test-battle She can throw at me. I feel like I can live forever! I wake up each morning really rested and ready for whatever battle is on today!' He grinned like a five-year-old, too!

Meet life's problems head-on!

A positive way to use up adrenalin is to win a few battles by tackling life and the problems it throws at you; the negative way is to stay awake all night, muscles rigid and adrenally-saturated still, because you've tackled no tasks, done nothing, lost every battle and are now lying there worrying about everything.

These athletes are fit, meeting the challenge of the race magnificently. Use up adrenalin by *winning* battles.

Fear, anxiety, apprehension, panic, even over-concern, all whip adrenalin out into the bloodstream, too. Use it up by winning battles, understanding that this is the real way of nature, and find yourself incredibly ready to relax quickly and deeply, in floppy sleep, restoring enough adrenalin to get you springing out of bed ready for the next battle every morning.

Or would you rather take your Valium and suffer a reduced ability to fight back (even against major diseases!) so that even the thought of a battle has you tearing off another pill from that foil strip?

Another marijuana cigarette will have an even more permanent and long-term, destructive effect. Not only will you reduce your ability to fight back, against diseases as well as against circumstances, but you'll be *so* relaxed you won't even hear the everyday battle calls, let alone respond to them, when life sends out a challenge which you must overcome in order to survive! A great race of Lotus-eaters we would become, singing and smiling as the vines grew over our faces, the wrens nested in our hair and we waited for the government to do something!

Many people mistakenly believe nature to be a gentle, reliable supplier of natural crutches to we poor humans. The truth is gained after hard experience. Adrenalin, that 'fight or flight' hormone, is needed now more than ever before, if all western civilisation's contributions to life are to be preserved. Are *you* going to fight, or will you run away, waiting out your life in a haze of relaxation-producing agents and creeds, having it all happen *to* you, a passenger, not a driver?

So now we have looked a little deeper at this 'hypertension', do you see how it frustrates and inhibits those fight mechanisms? The only one getting hurt is you, as you sit or lie down and try vainly to relax. Learn another of nature's balances: it is more difficult to rest if you have not experienced a challenge. Hearts are strengthened and rested again by muscle-mindedness, not by tranquillisers. *Do* something: don't just worry about it.

For those people who still demand crutches instead of using their own legs, there are a few natural supports: vitamin B_3, which can trigger off noradrenalin, and vitamin B_6, which balances its production and use. When your muscles harden and you tense up to meet (and survive!) a challenge, vitamins B_3 and B_6 monitor the signals from brain and adrenal hormones to tell you when the fight's over and you can relax completely again.

Increased vitamin C will ensure that eyes and adrenal glands, in which major concentrations of it can be found, are well supplied and have reserves available to meet sudden stresses, should they occur. Vitamin E and iron both need to be fully supplied too, so that oxygen, that powerful shield for your strong right arm, can give you stamina and endurance.

Many of our present-day youth are denied the satisfaction of accomplishing something. They start life licked! Are the battles really tougher now? Then why do we have so much emphasis on leisure industries, gadgets, technology and science to lull us into believing life is really a pleasant pastime while we wait for death? We are told that the battles are theoretically *easier* now than at any other time in history, science has looked after us and technology has enabled science to be put to practical use.

Nature tells us differently, however, and so does the 'modern' disease called hypertension. When pent-up adrenalin boils up, violence, terrorism, wars and racial brawls must result. Individuals can stop this happening: use your adrenalin to *act*; don't leave it in muscles and bloodstream and through the heart, for that way we die younger and younger, or find ourselves propped up by pills and science for our three score years and ten, wondering vaguely why we feel so dissatisfied with our lives.

Hearty, we call a truly genial, happy person. Yet you may find behind him or her a history of traumas survived, obstacles overcome and challenges won that fills you with admiration. 'I'd love to be self-sufficient, self-confident, strong and on top like you,' you say. Well, they weren't born like that; they made it happen.

Oxygen gives you stamina, and endurance – think of it as a powerful shield for your right arm, an armour against stress!

Arteries and veins

The two partners involved in circulation of the blood through the body, the arteries and veins, used to glue me to anatomy books while I marvelled at the complex plumbing of red and blue that filled the body with a network of push-pull feeding. The pressure all through this system must be monitored correctly in order for it to function well and give the heart an easier job, but it is complicated by one half, the veins, being slow and operating at a higher volume and flow pressure, while the arteries are much faster, and although pressure can also rise under effort it drops again at rest. Here we see the arterial Hare and the venous

Tortoise, both trying to get to the finishing line, the heart.

If the arteries make it too quickly and venous return is too slow, varicose veins, haemorrhoids, thromboses and such-like will result. How to speed up the tortoise a little and slow down the hare often depends on blood viscosity and a third party, the lymphatic system. We'll deal with this fascinating 'cold water' circulation shortly, but first, let's look at the tortoise problem, how to safely speed up the venous blood flow.

The slow circulation of the veins returns to the heart impure blood which has passed through tissues and organs, and now needs cleaning. The lungs provide more oxygen and remove carbon dioxide wastes, 'cleaning' the blood by increasing its oxygen-carrying ability. That's why the slower, venous blood is bluer, almost purple – it lacks oxygen – in contrast to arterial blood, which is bright red and faster flowing at a higher pressure. You can bleed like a stuck pig from an artery, whereas from veins you seep slowly and even imperceptibly. Little evidence of haemorrhages and pressure may show around veins, where thromboses (or clots) can form years before any symptoms of their presence are noticed. Whereas you'll know all about what your arteries are doing, your veins can break down much more secretively.

Varicose veins

The causes of the more obvious vein disturbances, varicose bulging and thickening, may date back ten or twenty years before the day you say to your health practitioner: 'I've got varicose veins; how can I get rid of them?' By the time you have that conversation, there's a long treatment ahead of you, because the time to do things differently was twenty or thirty years before, and there is no quick, five-minute cure.

I explain it by likening healthy veins to a straight-banked, deep river moving along at a full but steady pace, compared to the winding, serpentine course of a stream where every bend is clogged and slowed-down by sandbanks, where the water-flow is sluggish and dramatically less clean. Trying to turn that second stream into something like the first one will involve time. Those slow corners will need to be dredged clear and the stream's banks will need to be reinforced in order to stand up to the gradual return to a more powerful current.

Varicose veins are like the course of a river where every bend is clogged and slowed down by a build-up of silt. Trying to turn that river into one which flows at a steady pace means that slow corners will need to be dredged clear, and the stream's banks reinforced.

Varicose veins may take many years to improve – exercise, lecithin, vitamin E and rutin notwithstanding. There is a massive reconstruction job needed, and you can't dam the river and do it quickly! The circulation must continue safely, while you're re-arranging those venous channels.

So don't expect miraculous improvement with varicosity from *any* health professional. Perhaps your choice of parents and grandparents left something to be desired! Varicose veins tend to run in the family, so it may not only be your life-style and nutrition that was wrong, but your mother's and your grandmother's before her!

A family history which shows that members tend to have low arterial blood pressure suggests that future generations are also likely to have varicose problems. Think of the logic of this for a moment. The *lower* the arterial pressure, the *slower* will be the venous circulation. When exercise and effort occur, the arterial pressure can jump up quite quickly; but not so the venous pressure! And increased pressure resulting from fast circulation puts enormous strain on those slower veins. Often the venous river breaks its banks, overflowing *sideways* to cope with that increased loading. The first step to varicosity is taken; the venous river can never naturally flow as fast past that point again. The first 'sandbank' of fatty deposits builds up against vein walls and at the new 'bend' in the river the flow slows down.

'Stripping' varicose veins surgically is like sending bulldozers to clear the silted-up channel so that the flow around the bend will speed up but since nothing is done to *rebuild* the original river bank – the vein walls, after bulldozing – the next arterial 'flood' will damage those now-weakened vein walls in the same way.

Naturopaths are more concerned with diagnosing a tendency to varicosity early. Steps can then be taken before the flood occurs, not after the damage is done; for later it can be almost impossible to reconstruct the weakened veins.

In males, abnormal physical exertion – lifting or carrying weights which are too great – can bump up the arterial pressure too quickly and blow a vein in the process. Many later varicose patterns have showed up first at the end of a pregnancy for the female. The pregnant woman needs foods high in vitamin E in her diet in order to protect cell-division and growth in the foetus and keep arterial oxygen levels high across the placenta, but if she

When exercise and effort occur, arterial pressure can jump up quickly; but not so the venous pressure!

comes from a varicose ancestry, she should also take foods containing the two vitamins, P and K, which govern the clotting and anti-clotting factors in blood and maintain its correct viscosity. Don't let that venous blood 'thicken' and slow down when postural change and weight increase during the last few months of pregnancy force arterial pressures to vary.

Vitamin P, rutin, is an ingredient in many proprietary medications for the treatment of varicose veins. Sadly, by the time you are taking them, it is often too late to remove the evidence completely, but you can prevent further damage. If you add another two ingredients, vitamin C and the bioflavenoids, to the rutin and vitamin E and lecithin mixture, you will strengthen the vein walls against further collapse, and the venous stream will flow more freely and with less likelihood of flotsam clogging those bends. You may not have eradicated past damage, but certainly you can minimise the effects and prevent further breakdown.

Blood – the river of life

Blood is one of the most discovered body areas scientifically. The quality of anyone's blood is measurable quickly as to its contents and the particular 'extras' which tell much about disease mechanisms and the stages of progress of a disease.

Blood is pumped to every part of the body hour after hour, carrying nutrients and removing wastes. All cells are bathed in blood, and cell fluids and lymphatic fluids work with it in this constant feeding and cleaning of an otherwise inanimate structure. 'Dirty blood' is an old term once used even by many senior medical practitioners (as well as ancient 'naturopaths' who were often called witches or warlocks then!) to explain the reason for many disease processes becoming either chronic or malignant.

One huge class of herbal medications, the alteratives, contains plants useful at purifying blood, a term now quite wrongly denounced as unscientific by latter-day medicine. Alteratives are plants with a high content of sulphur, iron, phosphorus, chlorine, and many associated compounds which are used to treat specific types of blood 'dirtiness'.

If you read the chapter on the respiratory system, you will see how important oxygen is for maintaining 'clean' blood, and many

Circulation

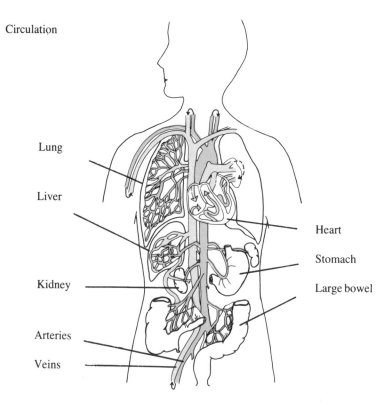

Blood is pumped to every part of the body hour after hour, carrying nutrients and removing wastes.

Lung

Liver

Heart

Stomach

Kidney

Large bowel

Arteries

Veins

alteratives have the ability to improve the blood's oxygen-carrying ability. One of the best known is garlic, which not only has all the above qualities strongly, but possesses cholesterol-gobbling talents as well. Now you know why garlic oil capsules, garlic extracts and tinctures, and using garlic cloves in food, figure so often in those naturopathic treatments intended to clean up and clean out many of your past sins which have affected your circulation badly.

The white flowers of garlic now used quite mistakenly as an emblem in 'witchery', black mass hocus-pocus and general devilment in the *mis*-use of plants to poison, inhibit and destroy body functions, was quite mistakenly lifted from its first emblematic significance. The garlic flower was the sign adopted by the first apothecary guilds in Europe and Asia, and it spread to many countries further afield as the knowledge of plant medicine increased. It changed from a sign indicating the local 'chemist', to a derogatory symbol for people classified as 'witches' merely because their powers of healing using plants were effective in removing illnesses! In times when sickness was regarded as a punishment meted out by God for some sin or other, man believed that the ability to *remove* illness *had* to be the work of the devil – and his helpers, the herbalists! It's astounding too, how much mediaeval suspicion of herbalist/naturopaths persists today.

The quality of the blood depends basically on the lungs and three other organs and systems: the liver, the spleen and the lymphatic circulation. The spleen destroys worn-out blood cells and maintains an immune-system which monitors white cell and red cell balance. The liver detoxifies, and tries to remove any inorganic sybstances which cannot be broken down by the body into re-usable combinations. The lymphatic circulation deals with the heavy metal residues and the inert synthetic substances like plastics, paints, environmental residues, etc.

The spleen

Another old term aptly defines a subsidiary role of the spleen. In Mediterranean countries it is said that there was 'bad blood' between people. In Iridology, the spleen feels the suppression of anger and violence, whereas the liver feels the brunt of suppressed emotion in general. 'Venting one's spleen' is inevitable when enough 'bad blood' accumulates!

In the physical context, an unhappy and violent approach to life emotionally can bring about 'bad blood' in the body, sitting in that emotional pressure-cooker! In the chapter on metabolic diseases, you'll see why cancers of any and every kind can begin in bodies where livers and spleens are emotionally disturbed, just as in the parallel instance where cancers can occur from 'carcinogenic agents' – a million or two of them – which make the jobs of the liver and the spleen at maintaining 'clean blood' impossibly hard.

The lymph system

The lymphatic circulation is probably the least-known of all body systems. Ask anyone where their lungs, stomach and bowels are and what they do, and most will answer accurately. Most people also know that livers are related to fats and alcohol and hangovers! But the working of the lymph beads, strung one-by-one on a chain, and in active partnership with the spleen and the immune system, are more difficult to explain. Yet, in the later years of this century, it is becoming one of the most important body systems by which health can be maintained.

Those lymphatic chains, concentrated around neck and thoracic duct in the chest, around the axilla area under the arms, in the groin and down the legs, carry body wastes away from each cell and then remove wastes by the normal blood 'cleaning' processes through the elimination organs of bladder, bowels, lungs and skin. Unless you empty the lymph channels of various tissue wastes regularly, lymphatic slowness, even stasis can occur. A lymph node can enlarge with accumulated toxins and wastes, even metallic residues or inorganic compounds, and a lymphatic 'lump', a tumour, cyst, or even a malignancy, can happen horrendously quickly.

Even though you may never have heard about what your lymph system does, and where and how, I would be willing to bet you have heard of lymphatic cancer, that racing-away type of cancer, where an apparently hale and hearty person can become terminally ill in a matter of weeks, without the body issuing previous warning symptoms of any kind. Perhaps you have lost someone dear to you this way, and astonishment, as well as grief, persists. Could such insidious creeping death have been foreseen earlier, or even prevented?

I remember how concerned my grandmother was about bumps and knocks and bruises suffered by family members. 'Be very careful never to get your breasts bumped or hurt,' she adjured us females. 'It may turn to cancer twenty years later!' Similar advice was proffered when over-enthusiastic work or sport resulted in sprains or strains and twisted limbs. She would massage the inflamed, swollen areas day after day, and make us exercise them until fluid was out of sore tissues and the joint or tissue was restored to normal size.

A good osteopathic chiropractor will give you not only five minutes of neck and back 'cracking', but a solid hour of massage as well, moving tissue about firmly and directionally to drain lymph channels, as well as tone up muscles and sinews. With that sort of treatment there is some point in adjusting the spine, because it will maintain its position much better in a body from which tissue wastes have been thoroughly cleared.

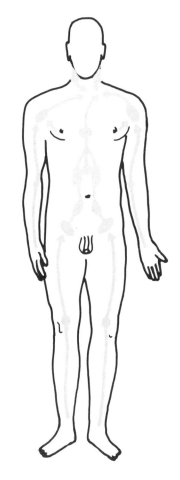

Lymphatic chains carry body wastes away from each cell and then remove wastes by the normal blood cleaning processes.

Is there any way you can check up on your lymphatic status? Do you have nicely-flowing, fast, rubbish elimination and therefore are you less likely to suffer from auto-intoxication diseases? Or is lymph flow slow (or, worse still, blocking badly in a particular body zone)?

Medically, the lymphatic system remains well-hidden until often it is far too late to clean and mend the clogged lymph channels. There are almost *no* recognisable symptoms early in the breakdown of the lymph system. A tumour or swelling, a lump, an enlarged or bleeding mole, may be the first symptom

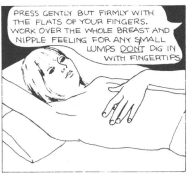

How to check your breasts for lumps – from 'Jenny learns about breast cancer and Breast Self Examination', *published by the Anti-Cancer Council of Victoria.*

Know the risks

First of all, know who is at risk of breast cancer. About one woman in 14 will develop the disease sometime during her lifetime, but some women are more likely to develop it than others. A woman is considered at high risk of breast cancer:

If she is over 50 years old.

If her mother or sister had breast cancer.

If she has had cancer in one breast.

Some other factors may increase a woman's risk to breast cancer, but scientists are not yet sure how important they are. A woman may be at higher risk is she has never had a child, or if she had a child after 30 years of age, or if she is overweight or eats a lot of animal fats. Continual breast problems, such as lumpy breasts, may also indicate high risk, but no one is sure yet to what degree.

Remember that the most important risk factors are those in the three groups listed above. These women should be especially alert to changes in their breasts.

Breast self-examination (BSE) is essential.

BSE performed at the same time each month helps a woman know what is normal in her breasts. Then it is easier to discover anything unusual, such as lumps, nipple discharge, puckering, dimpling, or scaly skin.

If any of these are found, a woman should consult her doctor right away. – from 'All you need to know about breast cancer', *published by the NSW Cancer Council* noticed (and as all the literature on breast cancer tells you, *don't let any suspect lump go unchecked*), but by the time this has happened, it may need massive and intrusive correction. This could mean radical surgery, because your body can no longer move cell rubbish away from the area, and auto-intoxication is complete – you poison yourself with your own toxic wastes.

So how are we to obtain early information about that hidden circulation – that deep 'cold-water' circulation as I call it – in time? One of the greatest blessings in the use of iridology is to be able to warn someone, maybe ten or twenty years early, that he or she has a lymphatic system which needs clearing, cleaning and smartening up. The Lymphatic Rosary, as it was called by early iridologists, will only be visible in an iris when the lymph flow is *not* completely removing all the toxic deposits from tissues. If such a picture shows in your iris, be those lymphatic beads pearly-white, yellowish or brown, an iridologist will give you early warning of your tendency to slow down at various lymphatic points.

Depending on the training of that iridologist, you will be advised about all sorts of correctives to undertake *now*, not when it is too late. Don't panic, and don't be misinformed about this registration of the lymphatic chains in the iris! All it means is that there is the *capacity* within you for your lymph fluids to move too slowly – for many different reasons – to clear cellular and tissue wastes away completely as fast as they build up.

You know when your bowels stop for a day or two; if urination stops for more than even one day. You certainly know, within minutes, if breathing out carbonic acid wastes is hampered; but you *don't* know when lymphatic drainage is impeded, unless you or your health practitioner recognises it in your irises.

Many irises which show lymphatic slowness show blood circulation problems as well. The lymph fluids act as a bridge between the arterial and venous circulations. If venous flow is slow and impeded and 'dirty' blood appears in arteries – a recycling process which shouldn't happen – the lymph vessels must work harder in an attempt to clean the body and take over part of the job. The lymphatic bridge also fills the gap between too high an arterial pressure and too low a pressure in veins where arteriosclerosis, atherosclerosis and varicosity have reduced clear flow and efficient cleaning of the blood.

Another duty for the lymph nodes is removing heavy metals

Lymphatic bridge

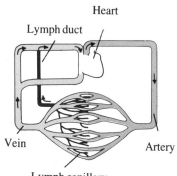

The lymph fluids act as a bridge between the arterial and venous circulations. If venous flow is slow and impeded, and dirty blood appears in arteries, the lymph vessels must work harder in an attempt to clean the body.

and inert substances like plastics and inorganic compounds, which the liver cannot break down into organic fuel elements, from the body. Have you ever wondered where such substances go? It's not all straight out to sea via the sewer-lines! First, they *circulate* in the blood and cell-fluids before being rejected and handed over to the lymph vessels to return to major elimination channels.

If too many of these impossible-to-use and impossible-to-break-down substances accumulate quickly, those 'cold water' drainage channels are going to become slow and clogged for a different reason. The lymphatic system can slow down to almost a dead stop if you are exposed continually to heavy metals, to many toxic ingredients absorbed through the skin and inhaled, even to hydro-carbons from overheated and overused oils in the take-away food industry! Do you wonder why lymphatic cancer and lymphatic clogging, and stasis leading to secondary cancers, is far more prevalent in highly industrialised, highly commercialised cultures than it is in third world countries and in quite primitive cultures?

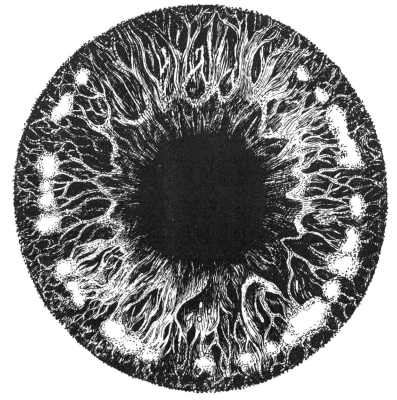

The lymphatic rosary – glistening white 'beads' around the iris rim –shows clearly in this iris diagram: a warning sign that rubbish is not being efficiently removed.

The 'cure' for cancers of this type is in the hands of each one of us. Even the knowledge of what so-called civilised living is doing to your lymph glands should help. What is the point of coming in desperation and fear to any naturopathic practitioner at the *end* of this process, looking for a miracle, a diet, a rigid positive-thinking regimen, a how-to-die class, vitamins, minerals, and magic answers to cancer? Come in twenty years earlier, and you could escape it altogether!

The immune system, that consortium of spleen, blood and lymph nodes, with advice from liver and mucus linings, is your best defence against any metabolic illnesses, including cancer. Leukemia (cancer of the blood and bone-marrow) is directly related to an inefficient spleen which, already over-defensive against possible infections, pollutants, carcinogens and metallic remains, over-produces white blood cells in a defence mechanism which unbalances red and white cell levels to a life-threatening extent. Chemotherapy attempts to reduce an over-active spleen's increased white-cell production, but in the process the normal immune system of the patient is destroyed and not re-established. A cold in the nose can kill a leukemic child, who now has no defences left.

Naturopaths are by law forbidden to treat any form of cancer. All we can do is try to support the body's own attempts to regulate its immune system. Iron is one of the most needed elements to begin that massive blood-cleaning process which may turn back the probable prognosis. Copper is most needed for lymphatic rejuvenation. 'But isn't it a heavy metal?' I can hear you asking. Yes, it is, but used in *vegetable form* as organic compounds found in plants, it meets the mineral *in*organic form with a 'like cures like' balance. Nature, far wiser and better balanced than any computer, had the answer thousands of years ahead of the demand. Almost all the plants and foods containing high levels of iron also contain the trace of copper and even the minute traces of cobalt needed to balance lymphatic flow and establish a peak of efficiency at rubbish removal.

It is not the purpose of this book to give detailed instructions on treatments to prevent or inhibit lymph stasis and possible cancers. And it is not the job of a good naturopath to bomb the body with harsh, eliminative, dangerous and debilitating regimes in order to blast out the end product of lymph stasis – cancers of several kinds.

We are exposed to heavy metals every day, such as petrol exhaust fumes containing lead.

It *is* the job of good naturopaths, however, to teach, explain and forewarn patients when their health is heading the wrong way. Iron, copper and cobalt: all are heavy metals, in one sense, but when in the vegetable form, they are goodies, not baddies, and all good blood cleaners, as are plant forms of sulphur and chlorine. But the most effective insurance against lymphatic stasis and all it can bring in its train is a simple one which most of us ignore in civilised living: hard physical exercise!

The lymph glands and another partner in the elimination game, the skin, are subjected to powerful pumping action during exercise. Not only do you begin to sweat and clear the cold-water circulation quickly, but the increase in body heat produced by exercise also 'heats' the lymph and burns up something else often stored with excess fluids in tissues: fats. Cellulite, that unsightly combination of fluids and fats that makes people floppy and flabby at an increasingly earlier age, is directly related to slow lymph flow and lack of exercise as much as to take-away foods and a high-fat diet.

Get moving! The lazy speed of many bodies is a direct pathway to metabolic and lymphatic reasons for different kinds of cancer.

A cure for cancers will never be found, because cancer is not a disease. It is the last defeat in a long line of battles which were evaded, missed or diplomatically settled. Cancers take half a

Cellulite is directly related to slow lymph flow and lack of exercise. Get moving!

lifetime or more in the making, and although those of the lymphatic kind can race away in their latter stages, that tendency towards slow and inefficient lymph flow may have been a lifetime condition.

So there we have our three rivers: arterial blood, clear lymphatic fluid and venous blood; red, white and blue. Being patriotic may mean more than just waving a flag of the same three colours! Its true meaning, from its Latin as well as its Greek origins, follows the same line of thinking as did the Egyptians who pledged their loyalty with clenched hand over heart, and referred to their own hearts, *Ab* or *Hab* by the name: Father.

Those three rivers of the body were reflected in nature, too, as the White Nile, the Blue Nile, and the 'Red' Nile (when algae stained the waters red once a year and a festival of the life-blood of Egypt was held as the flood brought renewed fertility to the Nile Valley). Our own three body rivers must also ebb and flow and synchronise their rises and falls so that body fluids remain stable. The River of Life continues by the same means as our own lives flow along and our bodies keep going each day by *movement* and *change*. 'Don't push the River,' state the mystics. Not if there is natural flow and movement, no, but when stagnation, apathy, passivity, even direct trauma like accident or illness, cause interruption to the human flow, life dies. You would die even earlier if life's rivers run sluggishly through you! Obey nature's laws of movements and you will live longer to enjoy it all.

7 Your Chemical Factory: Digestion and Metabolic Diseases

THE liver is the chemist of the body. After the all-chyme — istry (alchemy) that the stomach and small intestine perform on foods, and drinks, the liver must sort out from all this 'chyme' and 'chyle' (the semi-liquid substance in the stomach resulting from the initial breakdown of food) the appropriate new chemical combinations which that individual body needs.

Metabolic diseases are, strictly speaking, those in which the process of necessary chemical change in the body is inefficient or limited in some way. The definition is loosely extended to many other processes where only *particular* chemical combinations cannot be achieved, so metabolic disease means that there is some part of human chemistry interchange which is for the moment not taking place.

It may be that one mineral is sadly lacking in your diet, or is inhibited in its chemical change partnerships, and is throwing

Digestive system

The liver is the chemist of the body.

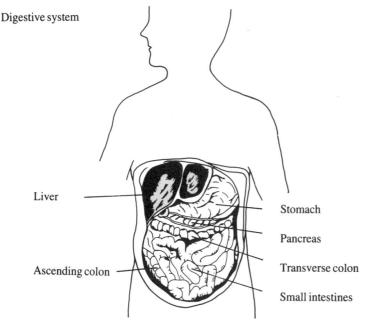

Liver

Stomach

Pancreas

Ascending colon

Transverse colon

Small intestines

out of normal function a body organ, gland, or even a whole body system. It may also mean that an organ, gland, or system is unable to use certain chemical identities because this body part has been damaged, is underdeveloped, shocked or otherwise traumatised. Metabolism is, literally, the process of changing, growing, using, converting and then changing yet again, which is the intricately balanced inter-related chemistry of every living creature. Changing foods into different chemical energy-fuel combinations is the way life maintains itself.

The liver: a chemical factory

Everyone's liver decides differently! If you have a dearth of, say, potassium phosphate in your system this week, because of a physically tiring weekend spent building a rock garden, playing tennis too hard, and cooking brunch for a dozen unexpected friends who arrived on Sunday morning, your liver must try to make this essential muscle nutrient from the 'chyme' available. If you already eat foods rich in this nutrient, the job is made much easier. But if you don't consciously re-supply this nutrient quickly, the liver must hunt through its body-stores and try urgently to make it by robbing other functions and structures that also need it or store it.

So that's why you're feeling exhausted, sore, bruised and hassled after a frantic weekend! Your liver may be robbing the nervous system, bony structures, even your digestion, of potassium phosphate in order to do the priority job. Far from being a cut and dried system of anatomical and functional identities which have nothing to do with each other, the body is an association of *compensating* systems. If one of these is overloaded, another will plug in to help it for a while.

One of the great diagnostic uses of iridology is that the iris clearly shows how well you are coping with various loadings *at the point* of loading, and what reserves of energy and beneficial chemicals are available there. If you can't handle a particular loading, various members of the body's partnership, reflex or opposite zones, will be called upon chemically, as well as structurally and functionally, to shoulder part of the burden.

The clearer your iris is of colour and structural trauma, the greater is your capacity to cope with loadings at their source, without needing to call upon auxiliary systems. Conversely, the more discoloured and structurally traumatised the iris, the more you must rely on support from compensating systems when various loads are applied. Until orthodox and scientific medicine practises on the *whole* body again, rather than viewing the 'sick' part in isolation, it must continue making intrusive and chemically horrendous decisions about treatment involving surgery or pharmaceutical drugs. Remember, one *part* cannot be sick without the *whole* body being called upon to re-balance, re-adjust and help it chemically, structurally and functionally.

The liver is often the key to overall good health. If it is efficient at sorting through its chemical building blocks every day, the liver zone in the iris will be clean and clear, and the whole iris will follow its lead. Old discolouration, brownish accumulated fogs and clouds of dark colour and yellowish blobs and spots can all be cleaned out routinely.

The discoloured iris indicates that your liver does not possess those building blocks it needs to make essential body compounds efficiently. It must vainly keep on robbing Peter to pay Paul, all around the body. You may get a headache and feel nauseated after the wrong kind of food or drink, a smoke-filled room or effluent-clogged city air. When this happens, your liver is frantically searching for some other body zones which can be called upon to help chemically.

It is no use your going for a liver function test and being told everything is normal. Your liver itself may be performing a magnificent chemical juggling job as the loads are applied, but unless the appropriate nutrients are replaced quickly and well from your food, the liver's ability to draw efficiently on all those reflex and overload auxiliary zones will be lessened. Worse still, if those overload mechanisms are being constantly summoned to help, your liver may be maintaining its efficiency at the expense of the rest of your body!

Alcohol; cigarettes; coffee; chemical additives to a food or fluid which has been fiddled out of its natural balance of ingredients; pharmaceutical drugs; industrial waste, such as air-polluting chemicals (many of which are highly toxic though unpublicised): all these ingredients of civilised living must be sorted out chemically by the liver. It's hard to see how any of us can experience really good health any more!

With a glass of something alcoholic in one hand and a cigarette in the other, you may feel more confident and socially acceptable, but your liver will be cringing!

It seems to be the chief victim of that current Catch-22 problem called' 'economic necessity'. If it is economically necessary to sell vast quantities of chemical by-products from the oil industry (where the majority of them originate) because so many of us must drive cars, fly in aeroplanes, own fishing run-abouts and heat our homes with oil, when does it become economically *un*balanced? When we're all in and out of hospital, that's when, costing ourselves millions of dollars in health insurance, worker's compensation and medical supplies and technology!

When will that reason of economic necessity swing the other way? When no one will be able to buy all these marvels if they are too sick to work, and too financially burdened by a multitude of high insurance premiums to pay for it all from their compensation money!

Metabolic diseases such as diabetes, multiple sclerosis and anorexia nervosa, result when this balance of payments around the body's compensating chemical functions breaks down. Where the breakdown occurs may not be the point at which the original overload was applied. The liver has been using some very fast footwork indeed to pass the various loads around for a long time, before a weakness impairs an organ or its function and the music stops altogether in this game of chemical musical chairs.

In diabetic patients it is fascinating to find that there may be *no* obvious iris signs showing in the pancreas zone in the right

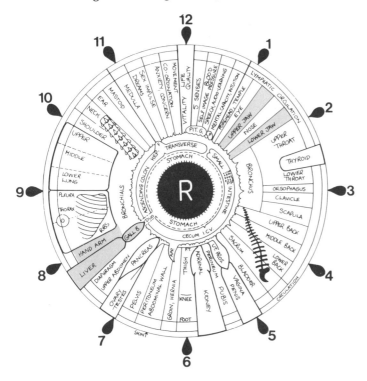

The impulse to put hand-to-mouth is one of the most powerful in the peripheral nervous system. In the iris, the right hand and arm adjoins the liver, and the liver is opposite to the mouth/nose zone. Think of twenty different behavioural patterns that link right hand to mouth on emotional triggers! Make it a party-game next wet weekend! I'm betting you'll find a *hundred* associations, not just twenty!

eye. There is invariably trauma showing in the liver and the adrenal zones, however. (As I have said many times to critics of iridology and students alike, the iris shows where the *original cause* of a problem is located, not necessarily the part of the body

---

Did you score 'kissing and holding hands' as one of your twenty associations of hand-and-mouth-related behaviour on strong emotional imput? Can you now also understand why new acquaintances shake hands and open their mouths in introduction? (Some cultures even rub *noses* and press palms against each other!) When a liver is supported by good emotional exchange, its task is much easier. 'Better to eat dry bread with friends than banquet with enemies.'

where systems have ceased to function later because of over-load.) These patients may be on massive, daily insulin support. Using the iris signs as a pointer, a good naturopath will treat the areas where the cause of their condition originated: the adrenals and liver. Insulin-reliance can then be re-assessed, as the pancreas drops a load which was never its own in the first place.

This is not to say, of course, that every diabetic has a whole, healthy pancreas and is only suffering from an overload else-where, but amongst the many diabetics who have been given dietary and supplementary advice at our clinic over several decades, only about forty per cent had an actual pancreas mal-function. The general improvement in pancreas efficiency once its partners who were the true culprits were given direct support, has verified the iris's indications.

By examining symptoms and the pattern formed by them at various stages, it is possible to trace diseases of digestion, absorption, and even of excretion, back to the liver and its efficiency.

It is just as hard to make silk purses out of sows' ears as it is to make good body chemistry out of poor quality food! If I had to name the most frustrating statement a naturopath hears from patients, it would be: 'I want to be healthy and fit, but I can't stand salads or give up coffee, and I've always had three brandies before dinner so that can't have hurt me. I haven't time for breakfast and I couldn't eat garlic because I'd *smell* terrible, and organ meats *taste* terrible. Kibble-bread sticks in my teeth, and

Magic cures are not new – magazines and newpapers always contain them! Today, many products promise wondrous results without being able to *deliver* anything nearly so wondrous. Keep your commonsense handy at all times!

raw celery is socially difficult, as is unprocessed bran.'

A thousand different excuses are paraded but a miraculous recovery, preferably within twenty-four hours, is demanded.

There is bad news in naturopathy, as well as good. The bad news is that you have to do a lot of it yourself. For too long humans have been demanding magic pills, not only to remove their ill-health, but for their need to change anything else required in their lives! It was the promise of miracles-in-a-bottle that made the travelling salesmen of last century rich – and gaolbirds! It is an unwise naturopath who will now promise more than nature can deliver! It takes time and mistakes to become metabolically sick; it takes more time to undo the mistakes and get better.

While bodies can sometimes respond amazingly fast if diagnosis and remedies are accurate, they still need to change their habits in order to make the 'cure' hold. Personally, I do not recommend that one take supplements or medication permanently, unless disease has progressed to the stage where irreversible structural or functional damage has been done. Choosing the correct support to use until normal function is restored ensures a stronger recovery in the end. Bodies are like children! Pander to every petulant demand and you'll limit their ability to learn *self*-support.

Perhaps you can see now why it is so hard to explain when someone asks which herbs are used to treat diabetes. Naturopathy can only be practised well when its philosophy supports each consultation. 'Every single person's *reasons* for getting diabetes are different; every person's treatment-support will be different. What suits one diabetic will not suit another.' The questioner looks disappointed, waiting to learn the instant magic formula that nature has provided for the condition man has labelled 'diabetes'.

When man learns that he or she may not make the rules, only observe those which exist already, there will be a wiser approach to medical treatment. If you, the patient, have been bucking the system and breaking the rules by which human bodies can function normally, there's no way out but to take heed of nature's disapproving finger, and retrace those steps.

Out of the pulpit now, and back to the practical! What you want to know is what to do about *your* poddy midriff, *your* few kilos of extra weight, *your* intolerance of fats, and *your* blood sugar!

People often eat their *traditional* food by habit, rather than the kind of food the liver really needs!

Evaluating dietary needs

For all metabolic diseases, I'd suggest a visit to a professional naturopath *first*. It's their job to sort out the dietary mistakes, mineral pathways, enzyme patterns and functional activity of that unique creature called you.

While Mrs Bloggs's liver may need chlorine, potassium and calcium, Mrs Angelo's may need vitamins B_1 and B_2, silica and magnesium. The only problem could be that Mrs Angelo was raised in southern Italy and is eating tomato and olive sauce and parmesan cheese over her pasta and Mrs Bloggs was raised in Birmingham, England, on boiled potatoes, corned beef and mustard. Both are eating their former traditional foods *by habit* – when, in fact, each may be eating just what the other's liver needs! Mrs Angelo can try every slimming tablet, appetite suppressant and dietary fad and still be voluptuously overweight; Mrs Bloggs can try all the same crash-course miracle slimmers and still have a torso like Boadicea.

A simple evaluation of their dietary needs can be professionally done by the new generation of naturopaths, who treat each patient as a unique set of rules which must be discovered and taught back to the individual. The iris will indicate which basic metabolic needs are necessary for a long-term, all-of-life programme as well as for short-term adjustment.

Who ever drew up those rules on the public weighing machines to tell you how much you should weigh for your age and height, I know it wasn't nature! The miseries many people go through in order to drop a few pounds take years off their lives! That liver which is juggling chemicals every hour of your life is also responsible for the chemistry which determines what kind of personality you possess. Have you ever considered that every thought you have is a chemical equation as well as an externalisation of your mind? Laughter is one kind of chemical happening, tears is another, and still your liver engages in its constant search for the balanced chemical equation.

Did you know that the chemical compounds found in sad and lonely tears are quite different from those found in tears of joy? Egyptian physicians did, centuries ago. One kind of vial was used to catch tears of happiness, another for tears of sorrow, and these liquids were used as medication for the person concerned when illness struck. Joyful tears were to stimulate, sad ones to sedate.

Almost too simple, too 'magical', for you to accept in the twentieth century?

The emotional environment

Self-regulation is a body's ideal goal, and it is accomplished in good, positive health. A huge part of this homeostasis is dependent on healthy liver function. That is why a hangover makes you feel wretched, or why hepatitis flattens you for months. And, rather more frighteningly, that is the reason our increasingly-polluted atmosphere, with its growing exposure of life to chemicals over the last few decades, is producing humans whose health is constantly sub-standard.

Just as every chemical equation produces a thought pattern and an emotion-potential as well as physical fuel absorption and use, so interference with your emotional stability can upset the function of your liver. It's that compensating reflex system of off-loading, again. You feel wonderful all over when you're in love. You (and your liver) feel the strain if you're sadly out of love again: miserable and off your food, or what is worse, eating compulsively to fill the empty space in your life – which is not your stomach!

More than half the patients who suffer metabolic shock or a disturbance of their liver function, and are therefore sick all over, are sick because of their thoughts and emotions, not from a poor diet or inadequate levels of certain vitamins and minerals. When most naturopaths ask questions about your sex life, your relationships and your emotional environment, they are evaluating the chemical load on your liver, not acting as substitute psychologists or psychiatrists. Your liver bears the brunt of unexpressed and suppressed emotions more than any other part of the body. It's a far healthier liver – and person – when emotions are 'up, out and over'.

You soon find out who really cares about you and who is worth knowing when emotional honesty is expressed and difficult situations are faced up to, leaving your liver free to do its regular, metabolising chores. A clear liver zone showing in the iris means 'what you see and hear is what you get!' A dark, stressed, congested liver zone in the iris, and what you see and hear will be only the much-edited version of the real personality, the real thoughts and the real emotions of a person who probably has metabolic disorders!

The high percentage of the population who regularly take tranquillisers, sedatives, mood-changers, pain relievers and stimulants indicates just how many suffer from defeated livers and whole-of-person illness. Nowhere more than at the liver is wholistic medicine more necessary. You can only be really healthy if your liver is allowed to practise its alchemy unimpeded.

Relying on pharmaceutical drugs to change the way life is shaking you by the throat is an admission of defeat, and you may spend all your days never discovering the personality you have the capacity to be. One of the most rewarding things I have found over so many years of practice and teaching is the look almost of surprise on a patient's face when, after following their individual plan, they have emerged from their illness not only not sick, but on top of life and calling the tune.

Good dietary building blocks and emotional equilibrium to make all those chemical equations easier to balance are two requirements, then, for the removal of metabolic disease.

Many of the major metabolic diseases have an emotional cause. Diabetes can start at puberty or menopause; anorexia nervosa hits hard at teenage females. Even systemic lupus can be traced more to emotional trauma than to a 'virus', as can multiple sclerosis, and – much more dangerously – many different forms of cancer.

The body's chemical balance mechanisms are upset more acutely by shock, grief, jealousy, greed, resentment, fear, depression, possessiveness and lack of confidence, than they are by a cream cake, a glass of wine or eating red meat! So many of the people who ask us at the clinic for 'a good diet' need hope, enthusiasm, confidence or peace rather than brown rice, yeast and vegetable juices. Even a good cry or confronting the person, the circumstance, or the emotional rack they're stretched out on would be more constructive.

Those to the far left of naturopathy insist that a rigid dietary re-arrangement will make everyone totally healthy and their lives a triumph of will power over temptations of many kinds. However, people following this regime die of cancer just as much as anyone else, proving that man does *not* live by bread alone, even the stoneground, kibbled wholemeal variety! Two aspects of health are missing in such beliefs: emotional nourishment and contentment.

Those to the far right of naturopathy allow you to commit every sin so long as you take massive doses of vitamins B and C, zinc, calcium, and enzymes, and many kinds of 'multi' and 'anti' formulas in handfuls of delicately-coloured tablets.

The balanced middle zones are where *real* naturopathy is found. You know perfectly well that you will drink a glass of champagne at Christmas or that you enjoy and will continue to eat a piece of chocolate now and again, when the craving for it sends out a shouted, instinctive signal. You *know* you cannot face removing tea from your diet completely if you like its taste and have drunk it moderately and with pleasure, for the last sixty years. The realistic middle-of-the-road naturopath also knows that you're going to keep on being human, too! The best thing to do, from the point of view of both patient and practitioner, is to pass information from one to the other about *why* you like to eat or drink particular things at particular times and what chemistry is causing such cravings to occur in your body. It is then possible to replace really damaging foods or fluids with others possessing a similar chemistry but less damaging an effect.

If you cannot give up all salt immediately, as a red-shirted naturopath or medical adviser has ordered you to, you can provide your body with a different form of those same mineral compounds it's craving by using *vegetable* sodium chloride. Buy a salt made from celery, angelica or kelp; it is still spicy and pungent-flavoured, but it supplies sodium chloride in a form which does *not* result in dangerous amounts of fluids being retained in tissues.

If a black-shirted naturopath (or even a scientific journal) tells you that the percentage contents of vitamin C in oranges and parsley are tiny, and that you would be better off taking vitamin C in a concentrated powder form with a vastly higher percentage, look beyond the theoretical 'laboratory tests prove' label and consider how human bodies function. Limited absorption time in the small intestines may mean that most of that undoubtedly excellent stuff will go straight down the loo, whereas a generous sprinkling of chopped parsley over your main course and an orange eaten afterwards make vitamin C more useful more quickly. Why? Because of the chemical balance of the other ingredients present. These various compounds have a built-in cell memory recognition resulting from people eating the same kinds of foods for thousands of years.

Obtain vitamins and minerals from natural sources – granulated kelp on vegetables and an orange eaten afterwards are much more quickly and completely useful because of the chemical balance of other ingredients present. Citrus fruits, alfalfa sprouts, chillies, capsicums and lettuce are great sources of vitamin C.

Allergies and the liver

What I call 'pseudo-foods' pose the greatest difficulties for our metabolic harmony today. After centuries of our livers knowing and recognising chemically prawns, onions, oranges, meat etc. so that each encounter with a food gives the liver no metabolic jolt whatsoever, we have now grown so clever theoretically that science can duplicate the flavours, smells, colours, and even the texture of the original foods. When we look at a prawn chip, our heads say, 'In here there are prawns and potatoes, maybe, onions, corn and wheat flour, pepper and salt.'

In fact, the chemistry presented to the liver after we have eaten that substance may contain virtually none of what our heads tell us we have just eaten! Is it any wonder that bright young medical students are choosing to specialise in allergies? 'Everyone is allergic to something!' they (and we) are told. 'Everyone has foods they shouldn't eat and substances they shouldn't breathe in or come in contact with.' Exhaustive (and expensive!) testing can provide you with a long list of things you should avoid; it can also make your life utterly miserable in the process, imposing a further emotional burden on your already worried and confused liver!

Vast amounts of information are available about 'the allergic response'. All of it tells you to *avoid* your allergy-trigger. Stay away from dogs, cats, pollens, house-dust, seafoods, corn or wheat products and artificial flavourings and colourings. So many despairing patients come to us for advice. Should they sleep in a tent, breathe through an oxygen mask, live on boiled rice only, and give up going out to dinner with friends because the restaurant will throw them out as unfeedable? Is bathing forbidden because soap may affect the skin? Will a walk in the garden cause allergic asthma to flare up?

They can be forgiven for lamenting that there seems to be nothing left in life. The quandary can rapidly become a quagmire of confusing instructions from all sides. Let's break it down logically.

An allergy is first recorded either by the liver, in the case of difficult substances, or by any part of the parasympathetic nervous system, that is, the automatic, relaxing, feeling, passive half of our communication and activity apparatus. When your body comes into contact with a substance to which it is allergic, it responds by releasing certain chemicals, one of which is histamine. This allergy response is carried to every part of the body by the bloodstream. Although the obvious signs of an allergy may be a runny nose, streaming eyes, a bloated stomach or diarrhoea, *all* of you, in fact, suffers the allergy.

The vagus nerve (tenth cranial nerve) is also a major contributor to allergy response. Starting at the base of the brain, it branches through eye and ear zones and sinuses, down through the neck and throat and across the bronchial tree and lungs, then across the stomach to the pancreas. Any or all of these zones can be affected by an allergy-producing substance, sometimes almost instantly. Eyes run, ears are constantly 'infected', the throat becomes swollen and catarrhal, breathing is difficult, digestion is laboured and enzyme function is poor.

Can I hear you recollecting that the pancreas is also involved in diabetes? The trigger for the onset of diabetes may also include a secondary cause, as well as the primary one of emotional distress, which registers in the liver, resulting in a new allergic response at the bottom end of the vagus nerve at the pancreas. It could almost be described as an allergy to sugar, and a difficulty in handling levels of blood sugar maintenance. Is your liver struggling under an emotional load, unable to metabolise properly, and being forced to throw out signals violently so that the brain has to sort them out via the vagus nerve? We can well ask if diabetes is just an extension of an allergy response!

Rationalisation has brought us to the following conclusions.
1 The liver is affected badly by emotional suppression and distress. Its other job, metabolism, becomes difficult because of this.
2 Psuedo-foods, man-made substances put together in new combinations, are new to the liver, and their metabolic breakdown can be impaired or delayed, or be incomplete, leaving residues which cannot be broken down.
3 Allergy responses occur when either 1 or 2 (above), or both, occur. Such allergies badly affect the mucus-lined areas of the body (eyes, nose, throat, lungs, stomach, bowels, etc.).
4 Mucus-lined body zones and skin come under the list of maintenance jobs done by the liver, anyway. A healthy liver in an emotionally-content body enjoying good circumstantial balance will make enough vitamin A to be used, together with vitamin D and calcium, to maintain mucus-lining and skin health and strength, and minimise any responses to allergy, even to less-than perfect foods pollution, food additives, etc.
5 Instead of food and environmental restrictions which are impossible to observe, isn't it better to maximise liver health? Isn't it wiser to keep foods and drinks close to the original, natural substances from which they are made? Shouldn't we simplify our chemical intake, instead of adding yet more man-made, 'scientifically balanced' formulae to our supermarket – even health-store – shelves?

Won't you derive more benefit from the exercise you get cleaning the house? After all, what good will a cupboard-full of instant detergents, spray-ons, wipe-offs, shine-ups, de-moulders and re-waxers do you? What's wrong with elbow-grease and whistling while you work? Your allergies may miraculously improve!

A popular television show amazed me recently by its insight into allergy triggers. There was that crazy field hospital with one of its surgeons itching all over from a violent allergy. It wasn't the mould in the jungle water-supply which caused it at all; it was

Do you now understand why you have sweets, chocolate or cream cake? If these were rewards as a child, eating sweets now can be a 'pat on the head' for the adult and if you're miserable about failure, after trying hard, you will give yourself a reward! But pity your liver!

re-living a former emotional shock in which algae and water were also concerned (an escape from a near-fatal drowning incident in a weed-choked stream as a child), which had triggered the liver into reliving the *emotion*, and producing the allergy.

Increasingly, allergists are finding from their experience with people (rather than from theoretical laboratory testing) that allergy triggers are firstly emotional; only later does any *substance present when that emotion is first experienced* become an allergy trigger whenever it is again present.

So it may not be the rolled oats you're allergic to; it may be that Grandma walloped you mightily as a child until you ate yours up! It's not a problem now, because you actually *like* the taste of rolled oats and enjoy eating them – but why do they bring you out in stomach bloat and an itching rash? Because you're recalling Grandma's overbearing authority, which you hated, that's why. See how the liver finds it impossible to separate emotions and metabolism? Whatever *emotion* is around when you are eating a particular food substance or chemical combination will invariably be partnered with that food substance for life!

Incidentally, do you now understand why you crave sweets, or chocolate, or cream cakes? If these were rewards for good behaviour when you were a child, you are now patting yourself on the head for being a 'good' girl or boy – especially if no one has praised you all day, and you feel slighted and overlooked. After all, you did *try* hard, so now you deserve to give yourself a reward. If you read all the good diet books and feel guilty when you eat the cream cake, see how confused your liver is becoming? Cream cake equalled 'good girl' as a child, but 'bad girl' as an adult! No wonder your liver cannot control your fat metabolism and digest the cream cake. It's still trying to sort out the *emotional* confusion!

Seasonal allergies

I do hope some of my readers are bright and awake enough to say, 'Wait a minute! What about "hay" fevers? Aren't they allergies? Pollens and grasses blow in the wind every spring: *they're* not new!' Some people sneeze and blow; their mucus linings swell up and breathing is a misery; their eyes run, and so on. What allergy-trigger applies here? Surely no one can be unhappy when spring arrives?

In the old, old books on plant medicines, you will often find a reference to spring tonics. One thing science has done is to analyse plant materials to find out what is in what, and why they have particular effects on our bodies. These spring tonic plants all have several ingredients in common; vitamins A and D, and iron. Early physicians and philosophers recognised the relationship between humans and natural laws, and cyclic and seasonal changes, much better than we do today. Much notice was taken of winter-type tonics and spring tonics needing to be different, because the body's metabolism changes with the seasons. Not only do the birds and the bees and the flowers take a slightly different metabolic and hormonal pathway in spring, man does too!

Dandelion roots and leaves have been 'spring tonics' for generations.

Spring tonics, consisting of dandelion roots and leaves, agrimony leaves and flowers and root, fenugreek seeds, chelidonium, seaweeds, nettles, etc., figured largely on the health scene thousands of years ago. There was a greater understanding of man's inter-relationship with the seasons, procreation, death and re-birth as nature moved through spring, summer, autumn and winter. In springtime it was necessary to wake up the liver after the long winter nights indoors when the diet consisted of stored roots, vegetables and dried fruits, smoked meats and salted fish, and prepare it for the metabolic change to springtime fare of fresh green vegetables and early grains, and the springtime emotional flowering of falling in love, weddings, procreation and active energy cycles. Hay fevers occurred if your liver was denied the different chemistry it needed in spring.

Today, you can give your liver (and progressively your mucus-linings, hay-fever, allergies) exactly the same ingredients whenever such body zones and resulting problems produce allergy responses.

Emotions and the immune defence system

There are a limited number of ways a body function or a structure can become traumatised. In the last chapter of this book, these 'out-of-function' resultants are explored more fully. Metabolic diseases fall into several simple resultant patterns:

Hypersensitivity → overstimulation → allergy

Hypersensitivity → overstimulation over a long period → hypofunction→ auto-intoxication

The first of these patterns belongs to the faster metabolisers; to children; to people with highly-re-active adrenal glands; and to those who respond quickly and actively by producing evidence of immune defence in the skin or mucus-linings. Those with an obvious and immediate response to a stimulus their bodies 'do not like' include sufferers from hay fever, eczema, dermatitis, and itchy, irritable rashes. Add to this group the catarrhal throat-clearers, and the stomach-bloaters with wind and rumblings.

The second set of conditions is found in those with the more chronic and deeply-etched patterns of major metabolic diseases like diabetes; allergies with no obvious symptoms except major disease patterns of 'arthritis' (which is *not* arthritis); headaches and nervous disorders. Even leukaemia and multiple sclerosis have been found to have a basic relationship to either of the above, in the many thousands of case histories detailing every kind of metabolic disease investigated at the clinic.

Emotional trauma is always present when that first hypersensitive reaction to a food, a fluid, or something inhaled or touched, is recorded. Either the immune defence system is trigger-happy (spleen, blood, skin, and *anger* and *violence*, either suppressed or apparently controlled); or the liver, in its major role of chemical factory *in vivo*, is assaulted by strange new food and drink combinations concurrently with suppressed, edited or unsatisfied emotions.

Our digestive and metabolic disorders are minimal if our emotions are honestly expressed and the emotional atmosphere around us is calm and peaceful. Instead of pestering your aller-

Often these man-made foods have names which remind us of *real* food-sources that used to be eaten by our ancestors, but the combinations of flavour, colour, odour and texture may *all* be artificially constructed by Man to 'fake' in our minds the genetic memory of *real* food. Our *livers*, however, take much more chemical 'convincing' than a well-presented package 'imitation'.

gist, perhaps you should look more closely at your own personality, and which of its perhaps painfully-acquired social politenesses and emotional dishonesties are contributing more towards your allergies than are dust-mites, artificial colourings or moulds!

In practice, I have found repeatedly that allergies respond faster, more completely and more permanently once emotions are sorted out, than they do to all manner of restrictive or controlled diets, or anti-histamine-type medication, or even to complex desensitising programmes. This is one reason why the B-group of vitamins is effective in the treatment of many allergy patterns.

B-group vitamins and allergy treatment

You have probably read in *The Natural Health Book* that B_5 is the anti-dermatitis vitamin; B_6 helps control many hormone functions, and spasms and cramps – which are attributable not to organic or structural malfunction, but to being 'up-tight' emotionally. Vitamin B_{12} is the master of the group – and where is it

Mouthwatering – and good for you! Strawberries, Stilton cheese, almonds, rollmop herrings and wheatgerm will raise your B-group vitamin intake as well as your spirits!

effective? In the *spleen*, that's where, and in the blood where all those allergens are now producing allergy symptoms. Even the vitamins B_1, B_2 and B_3 are spirit-raisers and enthusiasm producers, as well as supporting carbohydrate metabolism and liver function.

Now can you understand why so many books and articles advise you to take vitamin B if you drink alcohol, or have allergies? Read between the lines for the truth! Your liver is coping with emotional imbalance if you have to go out and get drunk to feel happy! Alcohol is the *last* straw, not the first one! The B-vitamins are going to help take the emotional load off your liver, and metabolising the alcohol then becomes a far easier job.

Alcohol and the liver

It is remarkable how some people can drink alcohol (often in quite large amounts) and never suffer any form of hangover. Invariably, these people's iris show clear, healthy, active liver and spleen zones. Invariably, too, they exhibit emotional honesty in their personality. What you see is what you get! If they love you, they show it; if they dislike, or even hate you, or are angry, disappointed, sad or happy, out will come the unedited emotion straight away, freeing up the liver for the business of metabolising that alcohol.

These liver-honest and spleen-honest people may prefer the wisest course of all: they *can* take alcohol – but they can also leave it alone! If such a person says 'No thanks!', when everyone else at the table is into the reds or the whites, it usually means that he or she is having a good enough time anyway, and doesn't need the extra crutch of alcohol to produce feigned relaxation and 'aided' good humour!

Hosts and hostesses often get the wrong idea if my husband or I wave the decanter past at table. 'Of course, we understand' they apologise, for quite the wrong reason. We're enjoying ourselves, anyway! If we *don't,* we leave! This kind of direct and immediate action is appreciated by human livers. Strangely enough, it doesn't lose us friends! As often as not, the rest of the table choruses 'We're not really enjoying this either,' and we all go off somewhere else where our livers can be equally honest about really enjoying ourselves!

For many males, alcohol carries with it an apparent challenge

There are no polite social graces about being an alcoholic. The accepted images of Man (a) *not* 'holding his liquor', and (b) 'holding his liquor well' are both wrong. Rather say (a) 'Man admitting social emotional defeat by killing his liver slowly' and (b) 'Man *covering up* his social emotional uncertainty by hand-to-mouth load-sharing with the liver.'

to their manhood. 'He can hold his liquor', was a phrase describing a tough, brave man. Television advertisements, especially, still suggest that drinking a lot is a manly thing to do. One of the organisations I admire most is Alcoholics Anonymous. Here you must stand up in front of others like yourself and admit to being a weak drunkard who has to rely on alcohol for a fake sense of well-being. There are no polite social graces about it. Your first step back from cirrhosis is emotional honesty – and doesn't that poor, hob-nailed liver appreciate it! Like compulsive eating, which I look at in *Iridology*, compulsive drinking is undertaken to fill a space in your life which is not your stomach! The first step away from the patterns of these habits is not taking pills, and having injections, or lengths of small intestine removed, but making quite radical changes to your life emotionally and circumstantially.

Another organisation that follows a good naturopathic road back to health is the Salvation Army. This time, the adrenal glands are the focus of attention. Are you going to fight or are you going

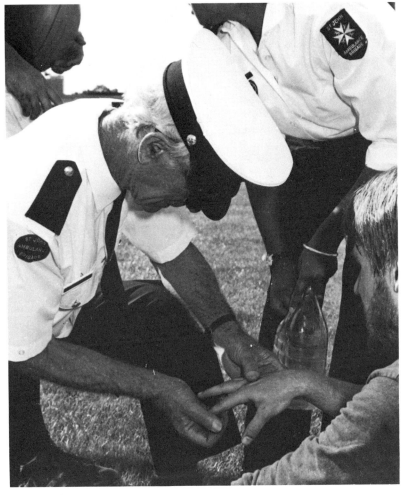

Two 'helping' organisations are the St John's Ambulance and the Red Cross. Their symbols have been like beacons in the emotional and physical dark-spots of life for millions. A *helping hand* from another human being can stop you putting your *own* hand to your mouth to stifle a scream of fear, pain or terror. Both organisations then send you off again, restored, for your *own* liver, and strong-again right arm, to wage the next battle – and win. *Neither* organisation supports you for life as a professional victim. Good naturopathy!

to run away from life's everyday battles? The Salvos recognise the battles with uniforms, martial music and enthusiasm-rousing sessions. Raising that courage again also raises adrenalin. Off you go with your shoulders back to tackle another challenge. If you fall again, defeated, there will be a Salvo there – *for a while*. But after a time, you must do it on your own. The Army doesn't encourage permanent dependence; your right arm (adjacent to the liver in the iris, and *sharing* the liver's load) must be strengthened by all means, but after that it is up to you once more.

Another ancient Order has for centuries cared for those whom life has treated harshly. Major traumas like grief, dreadful injuries, shock, horror, fear and panic happen in wars. The burden of such emotions are borne by the liver, the adrenal glands and the spleen. During the Middle Ages, the Crusades gave birth to the hospitallers, the Knights of St John who became satiated with war and its misery, and used plants from the waysides to aid the injured, the sick and the helpless. Simple field surgery began then, as did 'first aid', and so did emotional support to relieve the liver from a lifetime of later metabolic disease. The Red Cross and the St John Ambulance Order grew from the hospitaller beginnings. All support you *for a while*; all insist you then go off when strength returns and carry on *on your own*! Naturopathy, indeed nature herself, works the same way.

If your happiness still depends on whether or not you have alcohol in your right or left hand (liver- and spleen-related in the iris) look to your emotions before you 'go on a diet'. Do some honest talking and rid your liver, gall-bladder and spleen of some of those old bitter grievances. Emotions and metabolism are lifetime partners. Don't let one give the other a hard task health-wise for decades!

Reversing metabolic disorders

Now that we've grasped some prime factors which cause metabolic diseases, you can see that 'obesity' may equal 'resentments' etc., as well as inefficient processing of fats; diabetes may equal the bad 'space' you're in after years of emotional misfitting as well as an incompetent pancreas; anorexia nervosa often reflects sexual 'panic' as well as digestive impossibility. Any remedies I suggest in the following paragraphs *are part only* of the recovery patterns. The rest is up to you!

Harking back to those hypersensitive creatures sneezing, blowing and streaming their rash-covered, allergic way through life, a combination of the B-group vitamins and horse-radish tablets is well worth trying. Eat foods rich in vitamin B and have horseradish relish on the tables at mealtimes if you'd rather fix your problems through your food than through medication or supplements. It is no less effective, just slower. It will take 12–16 weeks on horseradish tablets to remove all that allergen material from your bloodstream. Horseradish used as a condiment thereafter can prevent the pattern of symptoms returning.

The A and D vitamins are part of every treatment which aims to improve liver efficiency. Cod liver oil capsules, or the gluggy emulsion, will provide an ideal balance of the two with quick absorption assured by the oil base (as they are both fat-soluble). Sodium, sulphur and potassium are also needed by the liver and pancreas, and vitamin C by the adrenal glands, and B_{12} by the spleen, and, and . . .

Wait a minute! What *isn't* needed for treating metabolic diseases?

Are you learning another truth here? The 'balanced diet', that hypothetical ideal which many of you are waiting for me to unveil: does it just consist of sampling everything?

You're not far wrong! It is as easy physically to fall into metabolic traps with extreme or exclusive eating habits, as it is with eating junk foods every day. Mono-diets: 'the steak and grapefruit' way to health; 'the cottage cheese diet'; 'fibre and fitness'; vegetarianism; vegan-ism; macrobiotics; the list is endless. All promise you a particular kind of improvement to your health pattern. Like the man says, 'You can improve all of the people some of the time and some of the people all of the time' this way. But 'all of the people all of the time' needs two com-

Eat foods when the time and the season are right – salads and fruit such as melon or berries are natural for summer, as is steaming mulligatawny soup in winter.

monsense principles to be applied. What may be a good diet for *you* is a bad one for someone else; 'good' food, nutritionally-packed in nature's simple seeds, fruits and green leaves, in roots, and in flesh of fish and fowl and animal, is better for everyone when it is served up as untampered with by man as possible.

'A little of what you fancy does you good', sings the Cockney. A *little*, not a *lot*! This refers not only to quantities in general, but suggests that variation may be part of nature's way to metabolic efficiency. After all, stone-fruits and grapes appear in late summer and early autumn in whichever country they're grown; squash, marrow and pumpkin is ready to eat during the cold months of winter; cabbage sees early winter through, too, but sweet melons ripen in the last days of the scorching heat of summer.

We're *supposed* to eat things when the time and the season is right, and our bodies have been imprinted with this genetic pattern for thousands of years. Man has become clever, though, and it is now possible to eat imported grapes when snow is on the ground, watermelons in icy, windy weather, and fresh berries in spring instead of autumn. The only way to truly 'eat natural' is to eat fruits and vegetables in season, realising that human tides go in and out as do nature's.

Do you really want to eat steaming mulligatawny soup in brilliant heat and sunshine? Or ice-cream in winter? Many of us *do* eat in this fashion, and in a way I suppose it is better than sticking grimly to salads all year round or brown rice at every meal. Variety helps the delicate metabolic balance swing up and down more efficiently than does monotony.

So get yourself a commonsense nutrition book and a recipe book to go with it, and forget about the newest diet fad or extreme plan for eating. A little of what you fancy, eaten with genuine relaxation and good humour, is best.

At a gathering I attended of eminent biochemists, allergists, pathologists, naturopaths, and other health care workers, we were all pounded with science and cleverness as various complex treatments for metabolic diseases were described. Then, later in the lobby, I overheard one very bright speaker toss off the gem of the whole conference. 'Really,' he said, 'you can do it all with a pinch of bicarb. soda and a spoonful of vegetable oil.' Shades of Hippocrates, he's right, too! But I would also add, 'and a spoonful of emotional contentment'.

8 *Listening to the Orchestra of your Endocrine System*

L IKENING the endocrine glands to orchestral components neatly avoids one of the chief problems associated with this major body system: describing it in simple terms! It's much easier to grasp if we liken it all to melody and counterpoint; tone and volume; percussion versus brass or even percussion and brass together; and describe the relationship between conductor, first violin and whole orchestra, than it is to discuss the complexities of hormones and secretions, and inhibitory and compensating endocrine relationships. You'd be gasping at (and bored by!) the intricacies of it all. Let's keep it simple!

Orchestral conductor	= Pituitary gland
First violin	= Thyroid gland
Woodwind	= Pancreas
Brass	= Adrenal glands
Percussion	= Ovaries and testes

and two hidden but vital orchestral components:

The composer   = Pineal gland
The score (music)   = Thymus gland

Having built your body structure (the concert hall) and filled as many seats as possible with vitamins and minerals, it is the endocrine system's responsibility to determine how well your orchestra plays.

On iridology charts, you will see that the various glands are prominently and largely drawn compared with the actual size of some of them to other body structures. The pride-of-place emphasis they are given indicates their importance in the function of the whole body structure. Have you ever wondered what determines when you reach puberty; when you start to grow (and when you stop!); when you get fatter, or thinner, or older?

Your hormones do, and the glands that produce them send various hormone communications to and from different parts of the organism as necessary, to maintain a *balance* of activity. When one or other of these glands changes the rate or type of hormone signal sent out, you yourself change. Your 'music' changes key, slows or speeds up in tempo, passes from one movement of the concerto to the next. The subtle and *ever-changing* signals produce the individual music of: *Concerto Homeostasis.*

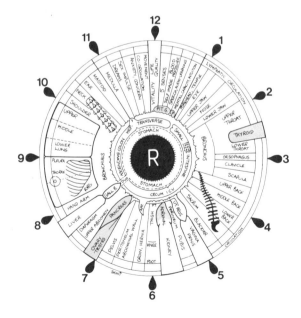

The conductor of the endocrine orchestra is the pituitary gland.

Pituitary gland

Let's first look at the conductor, standing before his orchestra. The music is on the stands; the hall is filled to capacity and waiting. The conductor decides how the *same* piece of music can be interpreted in a thousand different ways. Your pituitary gland sets your pace, or tempo. It decides how other hormones will be made and distributed, and the level of hormone production of each 'orchestral' type. Some people have 'music' where the brass predominates; others focus on the woodwind of the pancreatic enzymes and hormones; still others dreamily pluck thyroid strings and their thyroid ups-and-downs emotionally follow the *crescendo* and *diminuendo* of the string secton of the orchestra.

We all march to different sexual hormone drumbeats. Everyone has adrenal trumpet blasts from time to time. The harmonies and hormones of each individual change every minute of a lifetime. 'Hormone imbalance' is one of the hardest illness patterns to correct quickly. Up and down, up and down; the

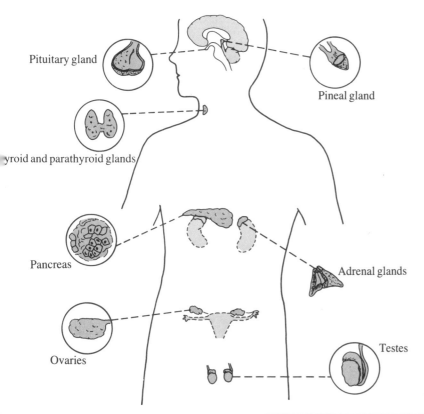

Pituitary gland

Pineal gland

yroid and parathyroid glands

Pancreas

Adrenal glands

Ovaries

Testes

Endocrine organs

harmonies change again and again so that no one agent can, or even should, be able to stabilise all the swings and changes of key.

Theoretically, the conductor-pituitary can control all the other glands in pace and volume. If, however, the first violin-thyroid decides to play faster or louder, the conductor may not only be *very* temperamental, but almost unnecessary for a time! So, in the body, a thyroid increase in speed can also cause *less* pituitary participation. The thyroid can take over hormone-signalling control to other glands for a time, and the pituitary may then even walk off the stage and take a dandelion coffee break!

It should not surprise you to learn that you 'feel' first through the pituitary gland the sounds of music heard by your ears. The emotional effect of different types of music on each of us is felt at the pituitary 'sensing' site. You can tell much about your type of pituitary function and overall homeostasis from the kind of music you prefer.

If it is Bach, Vivaldi, or even Dixieland, your pituitary-conducting is regular, stable and well in control of the predictable counterpoint of the whole body's harmony. You also have a well-regulated endocrine system. If the scene hots up a little towards Beethoven and Tchaikovsky, you have some thyroid-based mood-swinging coming up. If it's Valium-Muzak you like – background, non-intrusive stuff – your adrenal glands need calming down and your anxieties need easing.

And how can the disco beat ever be indicative of anything but disordered and strident, over-active and under-active glands

This oscilloscope will show the 'pattern' of sound on its screen. You have your own internal oscilloscope – you 'feel' first through the pituitary gland the sounds of music heard by your ears.

Those who dance all night to pounding beat and ear-splitting volume under strobe lights assume a cataleptic stare – and end up homoeostatically impossible to themselves, let alone the central nervous systems of their neighbours!

trying to sort out some order from the Coke-and-hamburger, pill and drug-induced metabolic mayhem our human orchestras must now contend with? Those people who dance all night with flashing strobes, pounding beat, ear-splitting volume and cataleptic stare, are homeostatically impossible to themselves, let alone to the central nervous systems of their neighbours, whose pituitary glands need calmer sounds at lower volume!

Is it any wonder that their bodies (and their cloudy, murky irises!) cost the nations untold millions in health care? 'The savage beast' (not breast, as often wrongly quoted) with nervous system in tatters, metabolism shot, and homeostasis permanently scrambled is too frequent a patient at our clinic. The age group of such patients is predominantly between 13 and 30.

In physiological function, the pituitary gland has periods of activity, directing the hormone-traffic, alternating with periods of comparative rest. Because of this, any medication taken to normalise pituitary hormones should be taken in courses of six to seven weeks duration, then not resumed again until a period of about the same time or longer, has elapsed. The conductor goes off-stage periodically.

This periodicity of pituitary function depends largely on each human orchestra's integration with nature's seasons, rules and changes. It is common to miss menstrual periods when travelling (thyroid); to put on weight alarmingly (or take if off!) when adrenal glands are active during anxieties and crises. It is easy to vomit when one exchanges motion and orientation on land for the different movements on water or in a car or train (pancreas). Man's integration with nature can be resisted or accepted. If you really believe everything depends on brown rice or 350 mg of vitamin E a day, you've got a lot to learn! Much more depends on how well your private endocrine balance plays in tune, and that covers every facet of your life, not just your stone-ground, wholemeal righteousness!

In the chapter on metabolic diseases, we learned how emotions are linked inextricably with digestion. The endocrine system takes 'overweight' problems one step further. It's a simple naturopathic principle that unless the *whole* of your life-circumstances are compatible for your orchestral-type to perform in, you can put on weight from hormone imbalance in no time at all. The really bad news is that this kind of weight is *exceedingly* difficult to remove! You can live on 500 calories a day and almost die from malnutrition, and put *on* weight!

Just like weight excess which is *emotionally* based, excess weight which is hormonally and glandular-based will not respond to dietary re-arrangement only. Circumstances need to be reviewed. The conditions which are throwing you out of balance may themselves need revising, even throwing out!

Back to our pituitary-Conductor, who has returned to the podium after the interval. *Light* profoundly affects the pituitary gland. One of the reasons why a stable man can be sent mad and killed in a matter of days in absolute darkness, with absence of *all* sound, is that this environment causes the total collapse of the pituitary function and therefore *all* balance mechanisms; chaotic breakdown of all functions follows. Grisly, but true.

Isolation from sounds and contact can *reinforce* the difficulty of the disharmonious orchestra present originally, which put the occupant of a prison cell in need of separations from other human contacts. *Not good naturopathy!*

Looking on the brighter side, that indescribable lift you feel during the first days of spring, when flowers and blossoms explode, birds sing and animals mate, is also pituitary-based. *Light* causes it; increased hours of daylight cause the hormones in plants and animals to increase in speed, volume and energy, and *your* pituitary responds to the signals of nature's Grand Conductor of Massed Bands, whether you like it or not. If you don't feel your heart lift in the spring, your pituitary-zone in the iris map is probably dark, murky and under-active. Life is not a giggle, but a bore; you're a Scrooge not a Falstaff! And, more importantly, you are trying to work across, not in tune with, nature's rules.

Not so long ago people wore hats everywhere. The hats came off after World War II (enough trauma in darkness *across* nature to warrant the renewal of pituitary function for just about everyone). Tonsured monks bare the top of their heads to gain 'light', a custom as old as history. 'Bald-headed men are sexy', may contain a different kind of truth. Pituitary hormones are definitely stimulated by light and the ultraviolet radiation from it. High, strong pituitary function stimulates the production of adrenal and sexual hormones as a result! (Jet-lag results from a combination of pituitary and thyroid disturbance, but more of this later.)

Several plants directly stimulate pituitary function. The least-known officially is sage. This common culinary herb packs a mighty punch therapeutically! It is one of the few therapeutic agents that can cross the blood-brain barrier and directly carry its high silica, potassium, sodium – even bromine and zinc – into brain tissues. I prescribe it for a host of pituitary-based complaints. Our grandparents ate it on bread and butter, stuffed roast meats with it, added it to sausages, drank it as tea and cleared their teeth with the rough leaves. In our clever quest to *defeat* nature and make our own rules – a doomed battle – we have forgotten it, but the Chinese have used it for centuries. That's where the Chinese 'sage' came from, as did the word 'sagacious'.

One of these days our 'musical score' may again be written from wisdom, rather than from scientific cleverness. Wise men of many cultures have recognised the pituitary gland as the seat of wisdom.

The second plant is better known – or perhaps it is better advertised: ginseng, that fabled, magical, esoteric, evocative vegetable root which has been used (and exploited) by those same wise Chinese who are now making a dollar or two from sales outside its homeland. The story of ginseng could fill many volumes, but two salient sentences are sufficient for our purposes.

1 Ginseng's prime therapeutic effect is pituitary stimulation.

2 Today's commercially-available ginseng bears little resemblance to the effect of the *wild* ginseng originally sought after and prized above gold by ancient Chinese empires.

That cup of tea brewed from a tea-bag with red-and-green-lettered 'Chinese' symbols on it will affect the pituitary gland far less than the real thing. 'You get what you pay for', is a sensible Chinese approach. One tea-bag can cost perhaps twenty cents. A perfectly-formed wild ginseng root, growing naturally at high altitudes in the moist mountain jungles of northern China and Korea and on the borders of Russia, glowing with a radio-active phosphorescence at night and loaded with chemically-safe iodine and bromine compounds, could cost you $200,000 — if it could be found!

Mild preparations of ginseng are now readily available in many countries. Do as the Chinese did: take it over a short period, then stop for a while. Like all of Nature's balances, there is a negative as well as a positive aspect to ginseng. If your pituitary is OK, or over-active, ginseng can speed you up to an uncomfortable level. Apply a simple test. Try some ginseng and judge your need for it on the results (one of nature's *easiest* laws to obey). If you begin to buzz about like a fly in a bottle, you didn't need speeding-up in the first place. But if you feel ten years younger, begin to lose weight, enjoy better energy and greater enjoyment of life, your pituitary gland has welcomed the stimulus of ginseng –

and you *did* need to walk a little faster!

Now you can see why so many claims are made for the plant and why so many of the body's functions are supposed to improve. If your conductor indicates the tempo of a funeral march and the orchestra has slowed down to a dirge, the music will improve all round if he changes to 'The Floral Dance'!

Thyroid gland

The two lobes of the thyroid are a balanced pair. Some of the endocrine organs come, like balance pans, in integrated halves: they work together, but separately! So do the tiny parathyroid glands, nestling in below the thyroid, and controlling, with them, many of the absorption mechanisms of calcium.

The skin, the hair, many hormone signals, the nervous system, and even 'arthritis' (or not-arthritis) depend on the thyroid's efficiency. This is the first violin, leader of the orchestra, who is quite capable of taking much of the performance on its own for a rehearsal period, but periodic appearances of the conductor-pituitary are essential.

Thyroid enlargements, the 'goitres' of yesterday, can be intermittent or chronic. Like the other endocrine glands, thyroid stability is dependent on all your circumstances, not only on your iodine intake. While many under- or over-functioning thyroids can be stimulated or sedated medically on maintenance doses of thyroid hormones, this is another instance where a pair of crutches may be unnecessary, if the circumstances causing the imbalance can be changed.

Periods of peak hormonal activity like puberty, childbirth and lactation, and menopause (both male and female) are danger times for putting on or taking off weight alarmingly. 'I'm *not* over-eating and I'm *not* secret-drinking, and I'm really watching the foods I eat,' may be quite true, but the situation is no easier to bear! The truth is that the thyroid is the most directly-related organ to how much *change* you can handle without Concerto Homeostasis setting in and becoming a disorderly cacophony! At times of major change in your life, thyroid hormones can be unpredictable.

The first time I went to England, some years ago, I put on one and a half stones in three weeks. No, I didn't drink English beer

If your conductor indicates the tempo of a funeral march and the orchestra slows down to a dirge, the mood will improve all round if he changes to 'The Floral Dance'!

and eat cold pork pies! I ate exactly as I had always eaten, but in that short period of time my thyroid went haywire. There are London doctors who call it the 'Australian disease'. (Equally, there are Aussie medics who call it the 'English disease'.) Many of you may recall suffering weight changes after losing a job, a loved one, or a pet. Others may have had changes in weight after moving to a new house, or from their country home to a job far away. Even marriage, divorce, or departing the parental nest to fend for oneself for the first time can cause this wild swing in body weight. Thyroid hormones shift the balance dramatically during times of major change.

So what should one do about growing thinner (or fatter) when the food and drink you are having not only makes no difference, but is not even marginally involved? Eat iodine-rich kelp, in all its variations, for it contains just about all the essential minerals and trace minerals, and so many vitamins, and it is marvellously compatible with your thyroid's needs. It is better, however, to take it all the time as a dietary condiment, rather than wait until it is therapeutically needed. (All seafoods contain iodine for thyroid health. It's a big argument against exclusive vegetarianism. If you really *don't* want to eat meat or fish, you *must* have seaweeds in some form.)

Don't wait to be caught unawares, as I was! Not only did the complete earth-flip bother my thyroid, but I made the mistake of travelling on a flight which gave me thirty-one hours of daylight all the way. I'm sure my pituitary has never recovered from the shock, although there's nowt wrong with it physically! Severe jet-lag is inevitable under this twin assault on pituitary and thyroid, and you may take months to recover completely.

If your weight problems happened at a period of your life when great change was swinging your harmony about wildly, your first violin was out of tune and the conductor was stone-deaf, then your performance may have been sub-standard for quite a while, and some of the audience may have walked out altogether! When thyroid hormones are upset, many vitamins and minerals are lost to your metabolism. Vitamins B_1, B_2 and B_6, as well as phosphorus, silica, and calcium may need replacing. The emotional instability, and *prima-donna* moods, tantrums and sulks, tears and anger (called thyroid 'storms',) will be greatly eased by adding these supplements to your diet.

As a herbalist, I would prescribe plants such as scullcap and

Don't try to administer your own medication! Consult your herbalist-naturopath for prescriptions to suit your individual needs.

mugwort; sarsaparilla, phytolacca and pulsatilla; even *Iris versicolour* (Blue Flag), for relieving the various symptoms of thyroid unbalance. Don't try to administer your own medication with these however. Thyroid-hormone adjustments are best left to the professionals. Consult your herbalist-naturopath for prescriptions to suit your individual needs.

The worst news about thyroid hormones is that time is needed for natural adjustments to be made. There is no 'seven-day thyroid diet', nor is there any magic speed about kelp.

Everyone must have tried to comfort others at periods of great change with that advice to 'give it time: time will heal'. Many of the Bach Flower remedies are of enormous help during periods of change: hanging on too long to the past; resenting your loss; feeling empty, bored or restless; losing sleep in nostalgia or impossible dreams; craving something no longer available, etc. All the 'Lot's wife' backward looks can inhibit your progress. These Bach remedies should also be professionally prescribed for you.

By now, hopefully, your first violin and conductor are happily in tune, in time and at ease. Next let us check on the woodwind.

The pancreas

I always try to avoid explaining about the pancreas. To me, it is the most complex body organ. We examined one aspect of it in

'Metabolic Diseases', and its function there, but its endocrine function is equally important. The orchestral balance between strings and brass is maintained by the woodwind: the pancreas lies midway hormonally between the thyroid and adrenals.

As the organ lying closest to your *horizontal* centre of balance, the function of the pancreas can be greatly disturbed by changes in your 'horizon level'. Every aircraft pilot flies on his 'horizon', the theoretical line that says both wings are taking equal thrust and the plane is flying without a tendency to veer off course. In humans, the pancreas is particularly vulnerable to motion sickness: that queasy slopping up and down of your innards when you go below on a yacht, or sit with your back to the engine in a speeding train. Your *direction* of movement in relation to other movement going on in your immediate environment is pancreas-related. The vestibular canals in your inner ear, your 'gyroscopic compass', tell you that you are 'off-balance'. Vomiting, a pancreas stimulus, may result.

One of the most obvious relationships of man to natural laws is our necessity to go in the same direction as the world around us. Remember those problems we grappled with in maths at school? 'If Car A is going north at 80 km per hour, and Car B is going south at 40 km per hour, at what speed does Car A pass Car B?' I never did work this sort of thing out. It made me feel dizzy just to think of looking out the window of Car B as Car A rushed past! Moving trains occurred in similar maths problems, and later, in high school, physics and vectors made me feel queasy immediately. It remained a fact that if I sat with my back to the engine, I would be vomiting out the window in minutes *as speed increased.*

Facing the engine, I had no problems whatsoever! Have you ever wondered why it is so difficult to walk backwards? Running backwards at high speed is impossible. Humans have a spatial movement *forwards* built in to them. If the container they're sitting in is going backwards at high speed, they have an orientation problem and this is felt by the pancreas.

We seem to have jumped from orchestras to trains! Let's return to the woodwind, that section which holds the tone and volume balance between the strings. Sweet-and-sour are the woodwind instruments: sharp, then mellow again. The pancreas relishes a similar food experience.

Let's return to those Chinese sages to explain why 'sweet-and-

'Perpetuo mobile' says the musical score, 'always moving'. But can *you* keep balance while continuous movement and change is going on?

sour' dishes began. Pancreatic *exocrine* function is better stimulated by a combination of tastes. Pancreatic enzymes of several kinds release better when first the bitter, then the sweet, then the sharp, is followed by the mellow. One taste pervading a whole dish is a pancreas stodge maker and can lead to poor digestion.

The woodwind instruments are mellow and sweet when those pancreatic enzymes are doing their job well, but the tones grow sharper and piercingly uncomfortable as the metallic flutes or rumbling saxophones begin! Wind blowing up or down in the digestive tract can not only render you socially unacceptable, but bloat out your waistline at dinner and ruin the svelte silhouette you arrived with.

Stimulate the enzymes with yeast or papaya, with alfalfa sprouts or alfalfa tea. Even horseradish or apple cider vinegar will improve the woodwind's tone and performance. Conversely, too much enzyme activity requires adjusting with chamomile or peppermint tea after the meal. But you will need the professional assessment of your herbalist/naturopath to adjust the woodwind's tone accurately.

Although pancreatic enzymes and secretions are more the job of *exocrine* pancreas function, the health and function of the *endocrine* pancreas are dependent on the state of the whole organ. Fennel, dandelion, fenugreek and alfalfa are all useful in both types of pancreas activity, but they should be prescribed accurately in medicinal concentrations if you have a pancreas malfunction. At home, though, an occasional cup of fenugreek tea, fenugreek and alfalfa sprouts in your salad bowl, cups of dandelion coffee and fennel seeds in borsch soup, sprinkled over rolls or mixed through cakes and loaves before baking, are easy and tasty ways to stimulate the function of the pancreas in *all* its aspects! Do you find it difficult to believe such simplicity can lead to good health? Prove it by doing it yourself!

Adrenal glands

The adrenal-brass blows trumpets, trombones, horns and tuba as adrenalin and cortizone put up natural defence mechanisms when man is attacked or threatened. These adrenal glands react to what was once politely called 'anxiety', and is now termed 'stress'. Both emotions are responsible for tremendous defence processes being mounted almost immediately. The trumpet has always been the instrument to sound the Charge! in battle: fear causes virtually an instantaneous release of adrenalin. How vigorous your first counter-attack is depends on adrenal gland health; how much resistance you have under long-term seige assaults can depend on cortizone production by the same glands.

How many battles do *you* win? More to the point, how many victories can you produce *on your own*, before you have to ask allies for help? How quickly do you fly to the pill bottle, or the alcohol or the packet of cigarettes, to help pump some more adrenalin into circulation? How much fight do you have in reserve for facing the battle after this one?

Brass bands and the armed forces of nations support each other in sustaining courage, excitement and energy, in order to maintain a strong defence and the ability to counter-attack. No one goes into battle on a Viennese waltz! Neither do your adrenal glands protect you from circumstantial, environmental, or even viral and bacterial harassment, if you expend all your available adrenalin on fear, apprehension, panic or over-concern. Such use demands constant production of adrenalin and its distribution, and results in adrenal exhaustion (commonly, and wrongly, termed 'nervous breakdown').

When the next *real* battle looms, all your adrenalin – your defence – has been used up worrying about whether or not it will happen! 'Don't shoot till you see the whites of their eyes' is not only economical with the ammunition, but has more effective results. While you are worrying frantically about something, it

The Salvation Army Band – the shine of the instruments and the rousing music stir the adrenals to march into battle! This organisation puts its effort into helping the poor and downtrodden fight life's battles.

may never occur! And even if it does finally hit you, your adrenal defences have been weakened hours, days, months – even years – before the actual attack. Think of all that adrenalin wasted long before the battle even starts. 'Cross your bridges when you come to them' is another trumpet and trombone phrase. 'Don't count your chickens before they hatch' is yet another.

Two positive benefits derive from the stable function of adrenal hormones. One is that abundant energy is available when energy is needed; the other is the ability to fight off disease quickly, completely and with a minimum of fuss.

The supra-renal or adrenal glands blow a brassy fanfare whenever danger or challenge is sighted. Why 'sighted', rather than heard, or smelt or touched? It is one of those body partnerships of an apparently unrelated kind anatomically which nevertheless has a naturopathic basis. The tissues of the eyes and the adrenal glands store major concentrations of vitamin C. If you see something annoying, worrying, frightening or just plain panic-making, the eye is the first watcher-on-the-tower to warn the adrenal trumpeters below to sound the call to arms.

Will you quickly respond and fight – and win – or will you retreat to the dungeons below and barricade yourself in against a long siege and eventual defeat? Your adrenal-brass and vitamin C levels will determine whether you have a chance or not.

Your body's defences will suffer if the trumpeter is asleep at his post and fails to give the alarm. It is plain disastrous if the watch-tower eyes don't even see the enemy approaching. You will be defeated without warning. Can you understand how necessary it is to maintain that daily intake of vitamin C? Whether it's oranges, rosehip tea, parsley sprigs, green salads and fresh lemons off the backyard tree; or a 'massive C' powder supplement that's your choice; in it must go each day to keep your 'watcher' awake and the early warning system on the alert.

Most of us have experienced the stimulus to the adrenal glands of a military brass band. A tapping of feet and a surge of pride, perhaps; a re-firing of enthusiasm and a will-to-win as adrenalin pours out, increasing the flow of blood to vital organs like head and heart and withdrawing it from the non-essential organ zones like the digestive tract.

Have you ever forgotten to eat when you were working hard? That's the adrenalin operating, hardening muscles in sympathetic action and avoiding parasympathetic relaxation.

Adrenalin gives you zing and pizzazz; it gives you enthusiasm and *drive*.

If you can't be bothered about anything and life's just too much altogether, your adrenalin is low. The danger here is not only to your personality but to your ability to fight off disease attacks quickly and completely. The louder your brass band can play, and the more regular the beat, the quicker the fight will be over!

Major trauma needs adrenal response. The reasons for the pharmaceutical use of another adrenal hormone, cortizone, may now be more obvious. Think of all the degenerative diseases: the wear and tear of old age, osteo-arthritis, rheumatoid arthritis, aches and pains in tired muscles and well-used ligaments. Think of sportsmen and women continually pushing their bodies past the point of exhaustion, yet trying to win always. Think of the massive trauma of excision surgery, when you're cut and bruised, and blood loss is high. Think of pain; just *pain*!

There are many body traumas where one can live with the limitation or restriction, but not with the pain. Can you now see the physiological sense in 'I'll just give you a shot of cortizone', or 'You'll have to go on cortizone, otherwise your ability to recover will be poor'?

A short-term shot in the arm may have much to be said for it, but there is everything to be said *against* long-term cortizone support. As with every 'active principle' isolated by theoretical and laboratory testing, this drug becomes a dangerously unbalanced ally in practical human use. What are its side-effects? Bones become porous and fragile as calcium metabolism is impaired. The adrenals are super-boosted at the expense of the thyroid and parathyroid's control of calcium distribution. The skin becomes mottled and resembles a damp, old, rough-plastered wall. The hair lacks lustre. The emotions of the thyroid violins and cellos become demandingly unpredictable. Many cortizone preparations cause depression and emotional distress in the long-term.

As always, the answer is in *prevention*, not establishing a permanent military brass-band pensioners' retirement village! If you've ever read books describing vitamin C's multiple 'cures' and wondered how any one vitamin could apparently cure anything from the common cold to terminal cancer, it should be easier now to comprehend. Vitamin C gives you more victories,

Arthritis in the making! Adrenal glands working overtime and therefore depleting rapidly. The natural hormone, cortizone, also running low constantly, and giving no protection therefore against skeletal wear and tear.

with the brass bands leading the triumphal march. It helps you to fight any major challenge, be it physical, emotional or circumstantial. Take high doses of vitamin C before, as well as after, surgery. Take extra when you're moving house, painting the house or catering for your eldest child's twenty-first birthday party at home. Take it when everyone else at the office has a virus except you – and you want to keep it that way. Take it when the shock of grief seems too much to bear. Take it after a car accident, especially if you're under-insured!

On the other hand, if your life is a constant record of victories gained in the face of every major challenge, you don't need heavy vitamin C support.

As the brass swells louder and stronger, the percussion begins; the triangle tinkles and rings; the tuba begins a gutsy bottom line.

The adrenal brass heralds the percussion proper, and several adrenal hormones are involved in sexual and reproductive music.

One female hormone, progesterone, is very similar. in molecular structure and pattern to aldosterone, the fluid-retaining hormone (an adrenally-distributed cue to the body-orchestra which keeps you from emptying out all your tissue fluids at every 'loo-stop').

Did you realise that the adrenal glands are basically responsible for regulating your fluid balance? Sometimes at a concert, you may have watched the trombonist emptying spittle from his slide, or the trumpet-player removing his spit-valve. The brass instrument player moistens his lips before his mouth touches the mouthpiece. Adrenal brass and fluids go together. Highly-adrenalised people can get very thirsty. They can go without food for long periods, but without fluids? No.

Some of you ladies who retain fluid before a menstrual period should now understand why. You may also realise why vitamin C (as well as vitamin B$_6$) can be incorporated in natural diuretic medications. Your body hasn't quite decided whether you're menstruating or needing to retain more fluids.

Menopausal or pre-menopausal ladies often have a terrible problem with fluid retention. As adrenal and reproductive hormones change, the aldosterone signal can become confused. Tissues fill up with the excess fluid, and out you bloat from a size 12 to a size 16 and back again; hormones see-saw unpredictably up and down for a while until your body settles into the more stable post-reproductive pattern.

When I am examining the iris, I examine the liver zone first, and check out the adrenal gland zones next. 'What amount of fight does this patient have?' I ask myself. Is he or she going to change quickly and positively with relief at returning health and energy? Or is this patient too tired, dependent, depressed, anxious and weakened, with a poor prognosis for eventual 'wholth'. Have all the battles up till now been defeats, or worse, retreats to cover, with not even attempted resistance?

One of my major objections to the increasing use of marijuana is that it lowers adrenal activity. You users may feel relaxed and that all is well in your human kingdom, but beware! You are lulling yourself into a false sense of security. Your weapons and armour have been removed, your watch-tower is unmanned and your brass band has been silenced.

'It's peace, brother,' you cry, as you welcome all kinds of enemies into your previously secure stronghold. There, they will undermine your walls, eat your provisions, demolish your structures and decimate your population. Singing as you climb the scaffold, you're a deluded, sick and silly sight. No trumpets are left to sound – and everyone except *you* could have foretold utter defeat.

Reliance on marijuana results in the user hearing an unreal story. (To the objective observer, reality is quite different!) You now live in occupied territory – your body – without even knowing you have enemies, let alone putting up a fight. You'll be tired, so tired, but you will explain it away as 'stress' and 'world economic conditions'. If you are sick, you will stay sicker longer, become dependent, passive, controllable and lazy, while the rest of us will pay more taxes to keep you – for a while!

I have never yet found a person, child or adult, who could not cope easily with life's challenges and disease attacks of all kinds more quickly and completely, when their adrenal brass is strong and loud. People like this get things done while others are still worrying, overcome by the prospect of expending energy on even small challenges. Life's a breeze, a giggle and a ball if adrenal glands are strong, fit, and full of vitamin C!

If you have a child who baulks at green vegetables, orange juice, or even oranges, and finds fruit a digestive chore rather than a refreshing break, checking the adrenal gland zones in the iris can confirm those instinctive signals as the correct ones for that person. Sufficient manufacture of adrenalin and other adrenal-hormone production can reduce your daily needs of vitamin C.

What about *over-active* adrenals? What about those trigger-happy active folk who sing, laugh, shout and yell, whose anger is up, out and over, who work long hours and love it, who whistle as they dress in the morning, looking forward to another fascinating day?

They sometimes pay the penalty of a different kind of allergy response. The spleen is also involved here, and the whole immune system may flare up to repel attack just a little too vociferously. Many of these strong, enthusiastic people suffer from skin itches and rashes or from sniffles and sneezes of the hay-fever kind (eyes and adrenals again). Their defences are always practising for the big battle around the corner, and they can run the risk of being stale and over-trained when one arrives.

Adrenalin which is always pounding out into the blood-stream when no major battle is occurring can put great stress on the heart. If the limbering up is taken gradually, not only can the heart handle it better, but the beat can become fuller and deeper, the heart can actually be strengthened and its efficiency increased.

If you stay awake, hypothetical conversations racing round your head, over-stimulated and over-alert, muscles tense and rock-hard with anxiety-produced adrenalin and lactic acid residues from the day's use, you will *not* activate nor-adrenalin, the counterbalancing hormone nature has provided in another perfect balance. Nor-adrenalin triggers sleep and muscular relaxation and is instrumental in restoring adrenal energy for the following day. If you sleep like your cat, dropping off the minute you hit the pillow and remaining unconscious until morning, you have nature's answer to your high adrenalin output each day: enough nor-adrenalin. But if you work hard, worried and concerned about doing a good job, then toss and turn all night thinking and planning, so that you are wakeful and restless at 2 a.m. or 4 a.m., and too eager to get going again, you are beginning a pattern of *over*-adrenalisation that leads to adrenal collapse, shaky hands, nervous twitches, the lot!

The 'rabbit-food' salad turned down as not manly enough for a hearty beef-eating male may be more necessary than you think!

All that vitamin C it contains (as well as potassium, magnesium and silica) may do more to build endurance, drive and energy than a heavy lump of animal protein. Remember, meat contains *no* vitamin C. The iron, the B$_{12}$ and the sulphur are certainly all there, but for vitamin C you must look to the plant world, not the animal one.

Plants as vegetables, fresh fruits, even some nuts or seeds are sources of vitamin C. A lemon tree in the back garden can provide enough fruit for a family, but remember to eat and use the lemons! Don't say, as many of my patients do, 'Oh yes, we have a lemon tree in the garden', but forget to use the fruit. The same applies to parsley, which is a rich source of vitamin C: eat it, don't just grow it!

When faced by a challenge, you can replenish your stores of vitamin C quickly with any of the 'high C' powders now available as supplements; but be aware that you are involved in a fight, and it should be *won*, not continued indefinitely.

People who may continuously need such support are those other crutch-users: the smokers and drinkers. In *The Natural Health Book*, the effects of these drugs on the body are explained more fully. Both affect adrenal hormones, and using them is an admission that you need more than the resources of your own inner army to meet the challenges each day poses.

In *Iridology* I also talk about the 'right-handed glassful and the left-handed fag' as indicators of emotional editing in social situations. Many people smoke and drink because they dislike the company they are in and would rather be at home in the garden, perhaps, or reading a good book, yet here they are, talking a lot of polite, boring rot, trying to win friends and influence people with scintillating wit, intelligence and charm.

I class this type of 'pecking-order' skirmish as a 'battle'. Adrenalin is needed to maintain a 'life-of-the-party' reputation. Cigarettes, alcohol, even cups of coffee, all boost adrenalin levels in the bloodstream – temporarily! By that tenth glass of whisky or the twelfth cigarette, the adrenalin level in the tank is dangerously low because it's all out on duty in the bloodstream. When another bout of stress looms up, you can't cope with it.

'Stress!' we all cry, 'The disease of the eighties!' Not so. If you'd been in that garden, or singing around the piano, holding a glass of apple cider or grape juice in your hand, mouth open in genuine pleasure and good humour, there would have been

Parsley is a rich source of vitamin C – an essential vitamin if you want to triumph over life's challenges. Eat it – don't just grow it!

adrenalin in the tank and some to spare when further loading was applied.

Stress equals *loading*, no more. As every engineer knows, everything has its load limit. Vitamin C also plays a part in helping us bear the structural loads applied to our frames, but in its adrenal role, it helps us tolerate the loads applied to our personalities. The social loadings mentioned above are far too commonly self-imposed, or we're told that they are necessary for 'business' reasons. I can assure you that every other person in the room is feeling exactly the same as you are! They're all wishing they were somewhere else doing something different!

Cigarettes and alcohol may help change their minds for a while; alcohol intake and ego rise together! Unfortunately, the more sober members of the party know what crashing bores lie along this ego track! Alcohol, cigarettes, and adrenalin racing out of control can persuade you that you're a combination of Marilyn M. and Mrs Thatcher; or have the males feeling like a Marlon Brando-John D. Rockefeller sandwich! You're slaying 'em! Except, of course, you are not – especially if they're sober!

True adrenal health blesses the owner with charisma. You knock them down with the real strength of your personality, unassisted. Your own internal brass-band is enough for everyone to hear your music loud and clear!

Feeling your 'stress' too much lately? Look for the reasons why in yourself, not in circumstances, for never has man lived so *un*-stressed an existence.

Ovaries and testes: the percussion

Those partying folk we have just discussed may pass the message on from adrenal glands to the next endocrine partner, the sexual and reproductive hormone producers, ovaries and testes. There is a chapter on the reproductive system elsewhere, but the top end of it can be activated somewhere through that alcoholic partying by sexual stimulation. The same story applies here too – you *think* you're feeling sexy, whereas the hard truth is that you are likely to fall asleep before you get around to it!

Let's listen to the percussion in this human orchestra, setting an underlying rhythm for the tune you play. Ovarian and testicular hormones are rhythmically produced, too. Males as well as females have hormone cycles. And it's much better to match two brass-band players than one brass-band type with one string quartet. In the latter example, percussion is hardly noticeable, except when the strings quiver slightly. But the huge bass drum of the brass band is audible a mile away!

Sexual interest differs from individual to individual as much as any other human qualities. About 80 per cent of couples seeking marriage guidance counselling cite 'sexual incompatibility' as a prime reason for marriage breakdown. Can you see how impossible it would be to blend a kettle drum and a violin; a flute and a trombone; a guitar and a trumpet? And yet many people spend a large part of their lives trying to force a partner to behave out-of-character sexually to suit *them.*

You won't turn one kind of person into the other, unless that person always had the ability to be more (or less) loud and percussive in the first place.

I've had so many duos in my clinic whose only reasons for mutual ill-health have been sexual. 'She's frigid'; 'he's too demanding'; 'I need more warmth but he's too busy and tired'; 'She's not interested, so of course I've been elsewhere'; and the mismatched music goes on, the percussion getting louder as anger, resentment, possessiveness, jealousy, even violence mount.

Let's slow down the beat a little and look at possible causes. The adrenal hormones hold some of the clues. Brass and percussion play together well, but if adrenal-brass really *is* exhausted and tired after physical or mental challenges all day, it will certainly be harder to raise sexual interest. If mum has been battling with young toddlers or a new baby (and the massive loads of washing and ironing plus shopping, meals and so on) she may be working far harder, physically and mentally than dad, who spends his days in cool air-conditioning and a quiet, well-planned office. Alternatively mum may be in the new, air-conditioned house, with gadgets galore and no children, while dad is working twelve hours a day selling, driving through busy traffic in a boiling hot motor car, in order to pay for it all. In community households, one sexual partner may often really be 'too tired'.

The sexual urge (not the act itself) is also determined by adrenal hormone levels. The sexual instinct is an aggressive one. More wars have been fought over girlfriends than over ideologies! If you're one of those adrenally-drained, alcohol-requiring

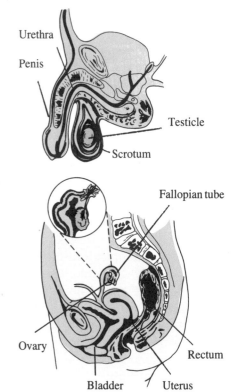

The ovaries and testes are the percussion in your orchestra. The sexual urge is also determined by adrenal hormone levels. Alcohol-requiring smokers need plenty of vitamin C to boost the adrenalin.

smokers, you may really *prefer* to go to sleep! Problems begin if your sexual partner is sober, active, and still bounding about joyfully! You may not need a divorce at all, merely vitamin C, less alcohol and fewer cigarettes.

If neither of you is prepared to meet on middle ground, the partnership is doomed. Sexual resentments cause more symptoms of illness than cancer. Why? Adrenalin again; the level in your tank lowers as you use it up in sexual battle after sexual battle, with none of them really won. 'Armed truce' seems to be a description of far too many sexual partnerships, and of far too many sick people!

If your bed is a battle-ground where one scores over the other with grievances, resentments, or unshared problems, the partnership cannot be successful and happy. One patient actually stated what many men still feel, although perhaps never say. 'I really shove it into her, the bitch,' he said. 'She's made me miserable for twenty years and it's the only way I can pay her back.'

How really stupid we educated humans can become! When sex becomes a weapon, we've removed our orchestra away from the conductor altogether!

The endocrine glands that should be doing our fighting are the adrenals. If you try to use sex as a substitute, you are admitting that your arsenal is bare of weapons. On the other hand, if all your other endocrine glands are functioning well and in harmony and balance, your sexual urge is freed for its true purpose – the pleasure of listening to the music.

Women are not exempt from the accusation of using sexual weaponry, either. 'If you can't beat the bastards, seduce them', has been the advice from unhappy mother to going-to-be-unhappy daughter, since Delilah and Cleopatra. Thank goodness our new thinking about women's roles has removed much of this image of the *femme fatale*. Unfortunately, we have much further to go, though, before we reach the levels even of some mammals! Satisfying the sexual instinct is not painful or traumatic, like going to the dentist, yet so many people refuse to indulge in its pleasure when their heads get in the way.

Whatever else you do with your percussion, it will continue to provide a rhythmic beat which will insist on being heard. You *will* feel interest from time to time. Whether you ignore it, satisfy it, take a cold shower, self-flagellate, or run round the oval, it will happen. To deny it is like saying, 'Food costs too much money, therefore I've decided not to feel hungry ever again.' Nice in theory; impossible in practice!

You can defuse this situation in two ways: you can write poetry or love songs, paint masterpieces or create beautiful things. You can also throw yourself into your work.

If a final parting has come, and you lose your emotional partner, many people do one of three things:

1 Have affairs with as many others as possible.

2 Try to do 1 (above) but find they are impotent (frigid emotionally)

3 Work long and hard

See how the adrenal hormones reflect the ego blow suffered by the sexual hormones? Do you understand how aggression and drive, diverted to physical activity, can even replace sexual activity most of the time? Not all the time, though. There will be those moments when a glimpse of two lovers hand-in-hand will cause your adrenalin to rise, and you'll want to thump the wall, or scream or cry in defeat. The sight (the eyes again, and their close connection with adrenal response) of your former loved one newly happy with somebody else may drive you to what the French understandingly call a '*crime passionnel*'.

Aggression and sex should balance each other; drive, enthusiasm and work, then relaxation and pleasure. Challenges which are overcome lead to peace, and then play.

Eye contact between two lovers. If that relationship breaks up, the sight of a loved one walking away can shatter the percussion section of you, sometimes permanently!

For several generations, we have seen an increase in sexual freedom. Now this is beginning to be replaced by boredom and jaded appetites, provoking some into seeking new sexual stimulus in as yet untried areas which might prove more titillating than those already known. Rather than exploring sex with pleasure and delight these same generations have involved themselves in sexual experimentation without good adrenal gland back-up, and almost out of boredom. The 'anxiety' generation has been followed by the 'stress' generation.

Those adrenal glands again! Depleted of adrenalin because of poor diet, lack of exercise, lack of goals and the drive to achieve them, their ability to enjoy sex has been even further eroded by a desperate search for 'satisfaction'. People like this are unable to win battles – what is more, few of them are even interested in trying! If marijuana is added to the list of adrenal-depleters, and many young ones use it regularly, it's not surprising that the western world is grinding slowly to a halt!

Is vitamin C the way out? It is certainly one of them. Of the thousand different solutions, every one needs that adrenal-drive to start it off. Be in there when it all begins to happen!

Any psychiatrist or psychologist will tell you that human behaviour goes wrong more often in the sexual field than in any other bodily function. Beliefs, ideals, ideologies and prohibitions, all tend to interfere in your *head* with what is really an endocrine function elsewhere. One of the greatest interruptors and restrictors of sexual activity is 'anxiety', that polite name for fear; another is 'stress', that polite word for weakness under challenge that we have already discussed.

Worry about whether you should or shouldn't, and with whom, still affects young people much more deeply than our enlightened education programs would indicate. A young teenager may have more theoretical knowledge of sex, and hold more sophisticated views on it than ever before, but when that first sexual challenge occurs, behaviour can be erratically 'old-fashioned'. The apparent blasé and bored behaviour can hide the same doubts of personal worth and attractiveness, the same fears of rejection, the same deep emotional storms of envy and jealousy that have plagued people since the world began. Sexuality may be talked about more openly, but the deep-down, insecure feelings are universal and familiar.

Every civilisation since the beginning of recorded culture has

Noise, music, excitement and a carnival atmosphere – vitamins B and C will help you join in the pleasure.

used drumbeats as signals. The faster the beat the more frenetic the dance, the war, or the self-hypnotic actions. Tight, active drumbeats can drive you to superlatives you'd never accomplish otherwise. The slack skins on the drums in today's pop, rock and disco bands are predictable, as is the blindly frenetic despair on the faces of the dancers! The taut, crisp drum-skins of dance-bands and brass-bands give a sharper note and an uplift to spirits and actions. Perhaps new styles of music can also lift world adrenalin! This may not be as over-simplified as it sounds; just think about the effect of one or two good, trend-setting new 'groups' on international morale.

What is your sex-*drive* like? Is it, as it ought to be, one of the relaxing pleasure-reward areas which all humans and animals seek and need as nature's balance for pain, work, struggle and fright? Or is it used as an antidote to help you forget all the lost and evaded battles at work or in other areas of your life? Have you failed to achieve work-satisfacton and enthusiasm as a result of battles you avoided?

People often say to me, 'I wish I had your energy to do all the things you do!' My answer is simple. 'What's stopping *you*? Is it fear, or hopelessness or despair?' (Vitamins B and C will help!) 'Or is it laziness or marijuana?' These two are often synonymous! 'Or do you want to spend your life on the crutches of alcohol and smoking, then beg me to fix your numb and useless legs?'

Our philosophies must change before true wholistic health can be experienced.

All those drugs which will supposedly increase your sexual pleasure and re-awaken jaded appetites will not be needed, either! If you prefer fake experiences, made in your own brain because of cell-damage and hallucinogenic metabolic change, and either slow or fast destruction of organs and functions, then you have denied yourself one of nature's major balance laws; real pleasure after work; real relaxation after battles won.

If the Aquarian age has any inherent lesson to teach us it is to discriminate between what is real and what is fake; one keeps to the rules of the natural sciences, the other regime tries to ignore them and encourage clever man to create other 'rules'. This is one battle none of us can afford to lose, individually or collectively. I do hope you'll be alive and joining in the pleasure, the laughter and the percussion's victory-roll. Remember that muffled, slack drums herald funerals and proclaim death!

Kipling's words are evocative and true. All of us march to individually different drums, but collectively, our percussion-rhythms, be they Central African, European, Asian, Latin American or Chinese, have a common theme: excitement. That stirring in the blood gives us new energy and renewed adrenal sexual-hormone manufacture. And what, after all, is our entire endocrine system all about? Balance. 'All work and no play makes Jack a dull boy'; an awareness of balance, that one, over-riding principle of the Universe, is the story of endocrine function and hormonal health.

When we understand this particular law of nature, we can see that it is a self-regenerating balance, too. What does endocrine health and good hormonal production do for you? It keeps you *young*! Within your body you have the means of keeping the whole organism running efficiently right into chronological 'old age'.

One octogenarian I know spends his time jetting round the world inspiring people to plant trees so that earth can depend on future oxygen-manufacture. Another sexy eighty-three-year-old can dance waltzes until the wee small hours, then rise at 6 a.m. for some hard ocean-racing on his yacht with one aim in mind: to win. My own grandmother bought an orange orchard when she was in her eighties, and insisted on 'young trees'.

'It's the future I'm working for' she told the estate agent.

If you have trouble summoning up enough energy to cope with the next hour, let alone next year, your endocrine orchestra may need to be stimulated into playing a livelier tune!

There is no one simple, natural remedy for restoring sexual drive. Magnesium helps; zinc helps some, and others need natural replacement of plant-hormone equivalents for a time, but an abundance of adrenal hormones will always stimulate those endocrine partners, the ovaries and testes into action.

Male prostatic and testicular fluids are certainly replaced faster when adrenalin is high. Females have better vaginal lubrication when they're adrenally well-stocked. The more you love life, the more pleasure you extract from it! Kissing a non-smoker makes sense!

The jaded, flat, empty faces of so many young people whose hearing and brain-cells have been assaulted by the mind-blowing volume of over-amplified music, and whose energy has been

Jaded, empty faces in the street. If you have trouble summoning up enough energy to cope with the next hour, let alone next year, your endocrine orchestra may need to be stimulated into playing a livelier tune.

sapped by drugs, testifies to their lack of adrenalin and general endocrine balance. Work satisfaction is unattainable. There is another form of allergy, affecting the adrenal glands this time, which will not show up until the 1990s. Associated with the parasympathetic nervous system this kind of allergy is concealed in organs like the heart and respiratory system, and in energy replacement. We will be living a very restricted existence in another generation or two unless endocrine function and balance is given a multi-million dollar research foundation or two.

So let your music play! If you don't care for its present rhythm and tune, change it! There are so many different yet simple roads to endocrine health that a professional visit is needed initially to establish each person's pattern. After that, a lot of it is up to *you*. For no matter which way you choose to give you good health – naturopathic, medical or any other way – nothing will be truly effective unless you also make some basic philosophical changes which will lead to an altered life-style.

The thymus gland

More revered and understood by ancient, rather than modern medicine, the thymus gland sits below the thyroid and centrally behind the sternum in the upper chest. Today's medicine has virtually ignored it, dismissing its rather large size at birth with a casual, 'It's associated with the endocrine system, but since it atrophies and shrinks from puberty on it must be of little use.'

More recent work by immunologists join its activity to general immune processes, especially auto-immune diseases – that is, those which for some unknown reason cause rejection of the body's own proteins and of various inhaled and ingested substances, and of tissue transplanted from other human donors. In naturopathic opinion, your thymus gland decides in the early part of your life what substances your body finds compatible with its growth and feeding mechanisms, and what should be rejected as inappropriate to human chemistry needs.

We have uncovered some strange thymus abnormalities while we have been working with radioesthesis and radionic hair-analysis during our research at the clinic. Some terribly disordered thymus glands have been recorded in children – those same children who drink kerosene, sniff petrol as if it is rose perfume, eat coal, and suck felt-pen tips and ends of ball point pens, yet who find ordinary foodstuffs are violently repugnant to them or make them sick. Have you ever wondered how animals and humans choose which foods and fluids are life-supporting and appropriate to their individual food requirements? The thymus gland, the discriminatory organ in early life, sets the whole-of-life pattern of choosing between foods and fluids that are compatible – or incompatible – with the organism.

One very strange child ate extraordinary things: pieces of carpet, mothballs, leather and kitchen detergents. He had a 30 per cent malfunctioning thymus gland. Many leukaemic children have the same distorted cravings, *preferring* to eat only one or two articles of diet, like spaghetti and coke, and nothing else at all. One would expect to find a sick child suffering from malnutrition and terrible metabolic malfunction. Not so! For that child, a 'normal' diet was potato chips! (The thymus gland was 40 per cent malfunctioning.)

Let's look a little deeper at these two modern diseases of leukaemia and autism. Both display all the symptoms of auto-immunity gone wild. In leukaemia, one's blood-balancer, the spleen, is over-balanced by the preponderance of white cells in the bloodstream. The patient's own body kills itself by auto-immune destruction of the blood, *by* the blood. In autism, the patient's own narrow choice of nutrients destroys many functions and restricts normal contact with others of the same species. Both diseases may be understood better when thymus function is taken into consideration. Both are primarily diseases of *children*.

In autism, the patient's own narrow choice of nutrients destroys many functions and restricts normal contact with others of the same species. It may be better understood when thymus function is taken into consideration.

Both are from 'unknown' medical causes. Both are *self-destructive* by the patient.

A normally-developed and functioning thymus gland tells us in infancy, through childhood and into maturity, what fuel is appropriate for the rest of our lives. A poorly-functioning thymus gland denies us this life-saving process. And what do we do to our leukaemic children? We give them a 'chemical feast' of chemotherapy for some years, using yet another, different, biochemic task, in an attempt to block out what is an abnormally functioning immune system in the first place!

> To each his own. A guinea pig doesn't suddenly become carnivorous, nor does a lion turn vegetarian for ethical reasons! Humans learn which foods are right or wrong for the organism from the comparatively large thymus gland.

Perhaps medical research bodies may begin to examine the reason for the thymus gland's existence in early life, rather than refer to its 'unknown function' after maturity. Perhaps, too, the vast number of children whose 'music' is quite different from the rest of humankind – different enough to kill them, or doom them to a lifetime of autistic isolation – may then have their thymus re-programmed with a more appropriate tune! For that's the part the thymus gland plays in the musical performance: it's the music itself, the score, written down so that each instrument plays its individual part in the entity that is the composition. Is it to be a symphony, or a concerto, or a strident cacophony of 'tuning-up' noise only?

Without an efficiently-functioning thymus gland, the orchestra can never play anything recognisable as a musical work. You would never get past the preliminary tuning-up stage, just as many leukaemic and autistic children never get into their Life-music, either. A jangled, irrational joining together of random sounds is all some will ever achieve. Sadly, we often add a further blast of chemical noise to the din, which is just too much for their human orchestra to cope with. The silence after it all stops is vastly uncomfortable to all of us who try to understand the *reasons* for illness patterns, rather than attempt to patch it up half-way through the performance by ill-considered, rapid changes in the score.

The pineal gland

Without the score, the orchestra can play only random noise, but many musicians 'jam' well together in *ad lib* improvisation. Dixieland magic illustrates this, as well as many other musical forms. A group of skilled, experienced muso's can intuitively follow, lead, and harmonise with one another, as well as play solo in virtuoso breaks, *without* any written music. What enables them to do without that essential for most other kinds of music – a composer – and, even more essential, a conductor?

The answer is simple. After gaining experience and skill in making music well, each musician becomes his or her *own* internal composer and conductor! Intuitively, instinctively, their harmonies blend and thread through the overall sound. Their pineal glands are alive and well and living in downtown St Louis! Their pituitaries are thriving, too, with the music created *by themselves*! A human being has no need of *outside* regulation under these circumstances. Man blends the old-brain instincts and intuition of the animal kingdom with the new-brain skills of intelligence to know and to understand the results.

Science and orthodoxy would have us believe that the pineal gland is equally as useless as the thymus! Almost nothing is written about the former in medical texts. Esoteric beliefs and ancient philosophies extol its virtues and uses almost *too* fulsomely. Nature's balance, as always, lies somewhere between the two extremes.

> Animal instinct is preserved in humans in this gland, though in a vastly less useful manner than through the pineal glands of dogs, cats, and most other animals. Humans who *listen* to that still small voice within, have a great advantage over those who ignore it as 'irrational' or 'illogical', or even worse 'not proven scientifically'.

Your cat knows days, even weeks beforehand, when you're going on holiday and leaving it behind. Your dog may howl eerily just before a family member dies suddenly. Your canary knows when it's going to be a hot day. Even the ants 'know' when there's going to be a heavy storm which will wash away their nests, and they move *ahead* of the threat. Aborigines fled from Darwin days before cyclone Tracy devastated the civilised areas. Intellectual development of the newer brain can often be at the expense of the survival mechanisms and just plain 'knowing' performed by the old brain for millions of years. Animals have much larger and more active pineal glands than do humans.

The new brain finds 'scientific method' a rational way to approach life; the old brain says, 'Rats! That just doesn't work for *all* of us.' The new brain replies, 'There's a statistically significant result taken over a double-blind trial series for a large group of control and actual test units.' The old brain says, 'Who cares? I've tried it and it doesn't work for me!' The new brain makes rules and invents things and applies technology to tasks and challenges. The old brain says, 'It's all *wrong*!' We're destroying ourselves with our cleverness. We're breaking so many of Nature's balance rules by which *everything* works, that we'll all die together, with somebody taking double-blind tests on how fast the destruction is happening!'

Children understand all about 'knowing'. Unfortunately, we then try to teach them a completely different set of man-made rules and expect them to adhere obediently to them. 'I hate Grandma because she's mean and hurts me,' screams out the child's old brain. 'Love your Grandma because she is your Grandma and you should love her,' is the newer brain's task to learn. 'That whole deal smells a bit funny to me,' you say, later, as an adult, copying your cat's investigation of his evening meal before deciding whether or not it's suitable and safe for him to eat. Your newer brain, your accountant, your bank manager and your father may *all* approve of it, and advise you intellectually that it's a marvellous proposition. Which brain will you listen to?

Fortunately, Nature puts her rules and balance mechanisms openly on display for those who wish to *know* rather than take an educated guess. In the iris of each human eye is a small area given to registration of the kind of pineal gland you have. If this area is clear in colour and good in texture, you should trust your hunch more than your rational approach. (You should also enjoy a jam session!) If the pineal zone in the iris is darkened by brownish blobs and fogs and yellowish stains or one of the iris 'special signs', like psoric spots or radii solaris, you'd do better to take and act on advice and intellectual assessment, rather than listen to any inner, still, small voice. It will not guide you well!

I'm sure every reader has experienced those deep moments of insight which are proven right by later events. A person you meet makes a profound impression on you and you want another meeting, and another. Or the reverse occurs. You take an immediate, deep dislike to a person during the first few moments of contact. 'Chemistry' it is sometimes called, but it is actually the use of your deeply instinctive recording, in a very 'primitive' way, of what is good or bad for your organism. The more one lives simply within the *real* laws of existence, the more one begins to compose and conduct one's own music, without outside help. Self-sufficiency, we call it. And it doesn't only mean growing one's own vegetables! It also means using those ancient genetic signals passed down through generations by the animal called Man.

Compose your *own* music: conduct its performance *yourself*. Overall endocrine balance, harmony and compensation can contribute *more* to your whole health and wellbeing than any other body system. It's the hardest to achieve naturopathically, though, because *you* are the chief regulator of your lifestyle; the stresses you choose to accept, the apathy of drugs, the crutches of pills and the horrendously inappropriate fuel taken aboard, are all *yours* to correct. Your naturopath can evaluate, advise and prescribe tools to help you fight, but it is up to you to do it all when you leave the consulting room.

My orchestra is tuning up for a great performance which gives me intense satisfaction, pleasure, hard work, peace and achievement! What's playing in *your* concert-hall this week?

9 *The Waste Removers —*
the Elimination Organs

Garbage bins need emptying regularly. Waste-pipes and drains need an occasional flush out with antiseptic, and a house needs its windows opened in order to air it, to remove stale gases and condensation. Even a child knows this. But many adult humans live with their bodies in a state they would not tolerate in their houses, cars and offices, or even in their garbage bins!

Bodies, like all of nature's living organisms, excrete unusable rubbish in many ways. Metabolism builds; excretion clears away the debris afterwards. Anabolic processes build too (flesh, tissue, storage of vital nutrients in cells), and catabolic processes tear down mistakes, carry away unusable items, and clear the decks for the next bout of building.

Even if you establish nutritional balance in your body with good, unprocessed foods and a stable environment around you, you can still be terribly sick if eliminatory organs do not carry away the waste-products which are inevitable from even a healthy input. Many old-fashioned naturopaths used to hit a new patient first with savage elimination mixtures (after fixing a censorious stare on daily 'bowel-habits') before they would even talk about present symptoms or enquire about your *intake* of foods. 'Eliminate' was carved inexorably across their foreheads. 'Remove all your sins' leftovers first; not until that is done can you hope to be healthily "saved".'

Even today, many natural-health practitioners and devotees place more emphasis on what comes *out* than on what goes in! Colonic irrigation literally 'washes' you internally if you can't do it effectively yourself, and fasting allows you to halt the intake and fuelling processes for a while and concentrate only on cleaning out the rubbish.

Both treatments have their uses, but a good naturopath will also look for causes. *Why* can't your body eliminate waste as fast as it ought to? What's wrong with the processes of excretion, or the organs concerned? Let's improve those, so that the real laws of nature will apply again; each of us should be able to excrete as efficiently as we absorb.

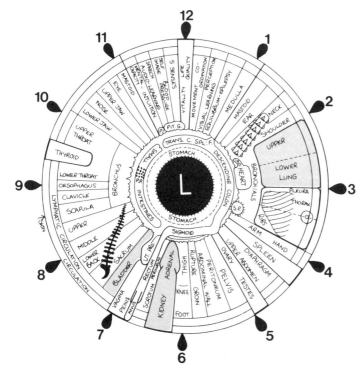

The rubbish bins need regular emptying and cleaning.

Iris colours, rather than shapes, indicate clearly how balanced our intake/excretion pattern is. On a blue iris, the giveaway clouds of yellowish-brown or darker brown, or the streaks of Radii Solaris (see *Iridology*) indicate a simple condition: rubbish is accumulating in the body faster than it can be thrown out. Many people with 'hazel'-coloured eyes, who are of European origin, would be astounded to see that the iris under magnification shows how their blue, healthy ancestry has been cluttered up by slow elimination. After the quicker herbal and homoeopathic treatments or slower dietary changes and improvements, they can also be astounded to find that their iris colour is visibly different to that of their family and friends.

'But I've *always* had hazel eyes,' they say, dazedly, after a couple of visits.

'How's your energy and outlook on life now?' I counter.

'I feel tremendous' is the reply. 'I didn't know it was really possible to feel so much oomph and energy, or to bound out of bed and look forward to my day. I feel *lighter*, somehow! Nothing is an *effort* anymore.' And all this has been achieved on nothing more than a thorough rubbish cleanup!

In those who have brown eyes because of their ethnic background, the true dark brown pigment has a quite different

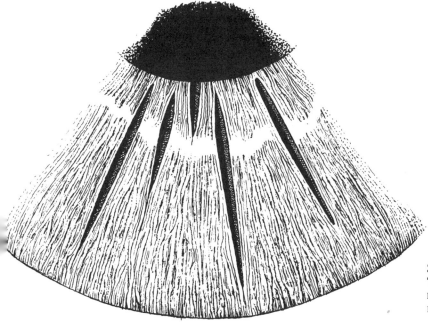

Streaks of radii solaris indicate that 'rubbish' is being recycled, even re-digested; this is destructive, even negative, nutrition.

appearance, like brown velvet. No white fibres show in these irises at all, unlike those irises of white Caucasian ancestry. Although iridology was known to and used by the Chinese, the Hebrews and the Egyptians (and possibly other races as well), I believe this to be one of the reasons why these basically brown-pigmented races did not find it so useful a diagnostic tool. But in those races whose irises have basically blue pigment, any super-imposed, brownish discolouration indicates a simple need to overcome sluggish organs of excretion.

The irises of those hazel-eyed folk may reveal not only their own uncleansed 'sins', but also the genetic legacies from an-cestors who didn't understand the price nature exacts from those who disobey or ignore her laws. You may have inherited your spotted brown or orange discoloured irises from parents and grandparents, whose incomplete excretion caused diseases.

In radionic hair analysis, a field in which I am now re-searching and treating patients for many and varied ills, I'm finding that about fifty to sixty per cent of today's illnesses are genetically-based.

One wouldn't mate a duck with a deformed foot and one wing missing with a drake with intestinal parasites and bleeding diarrhoea, then expect the progeny to be blessed with perfect health! A plant with twisted fungus galls and discoloured leaves would never be chosen as breeding stock from which cuttings or seeds could be taken if healthy future plants were required.

Whenever humans have culled out the weaker, the deformed, the sick or 'different' members of the population, a great cry of 'Inhumanity!' has reverberated, sometimes for centuries. Humans are the only living organisms where the strong support the weak and the law of the survival of the fittest almost never applies – at least in 'developed' countries. The sick, the halt, the lame and the blind reproduce themselves and are often assisted to do so.

While human compassion exists, and separates us from all other life-forms, health-workers have to treat not only simple symptoms belonging to one patient and totally of that individual's causing, but also the genetic characteristics of illnesses and traits stemming from parents, grandparents, etc.

TB experienced unto death by a grandmother may surface in a grandchild as asthma, or eczema, or migraines, or a hundred other manifestations of an inherited tendency to illness. Syphilis in great-uncle Charlie may cause anxiety-prone 'can't cope' nervous systems generations on. Leprosy has not been magically removed from the planet, either.

Genetics ensures that further down the line there will be *tendencies* to illness in progeny, weakness zones or particular structures or functions which will be 'trouble spots' resistant to many kinds of treatments and baffling to diagnose!

Radionic analysis and radiesthesia remedies *can* reach down genetically, and such treatment can bring about incredible changes in iris characteristics as well as benefitting the patient, who is freed from much genetic 'garbage' which otherwise might have been carried through life. This is a source of constant satisfaction to my husband and me as we work towards and learn this space-age confirmation of the oldest rule in the world: balance.

'Action and reaction are equal and opposite,' is Sir Isaac Newton's third law. 'Every body persists in a state of rest or of uniform motion in a straight line unless acted upon by some external impressed force,' is another of his rationalisations of the laws of nature, which apply in every natural science. 'Intake and excretion need to be equalised and are opposite,' is a paraphrase of that third law applying to humans. When sick, 'everybody tends to stay sick in the same way, unless acted on by some external, prescribed changes to *reverse* this process' may be a truism, but this 'law of inertia' is a human hazard hard to eradicate in the process called 'healing'. Nobody *heals* anyone! The best that anyone can do is to start the pendulum swinging back the other way in a gradual change of energy.

Elimination and the bowels

Let's take a look at that natural law of 'inertia' again in relation to our bowel habits. I will never forget a patient whose answer to my question on bowel habits was a brief 'OK'. (A bad health practitioner is often tempted to take the patient's diagnosis at face value and not explore further. A very dangerous and *un*natural law has crept into orthodox medicine: 'Nothing is wrong unless the patient complains about it.' Not true! Humans are very much creatures of conditioned response.) The patient above looked quite surprised when I asked, 'What *kind* of OK? Once a day? More? Less?'

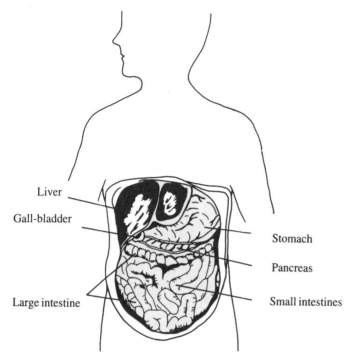

Liver
Gall-bladder
Large intestine
Stomach
Pancreas
Small intestines

The bowel uses natural peristaltic movements to empty itself of 'rubbish'. Valerian has no laxative properties, but it produces easy bowel movements in rigid over-controlled people.

'Oh,' she fobbed me off, 'I've always been the same. It's not a problem, really?'

Naturopaths need 'curiosity claws' to be really effective!

'What "same"?' I persisted.

'Oh, it's not what I've come to see you about.' She looked quite annoyed.

I took a deep breath and hung on. *'How often do your bowels open?'* (Short of leaning over the desk and grabbing her by the lapels, it was the most polite alternative.)

'Once every three weeks!' She let go of the information as reluctantly as she relaxed her anal sphincter! 'It's all right really,' she said, 'I've mentioned it several times to doctors and they've all said, "Well, if it's always been that way, it must be OK", so I've not worried about it.'

That law of inertia is responsible for more illnesses than centuries of plagues and the poxes combined! And what had she sought my help for? A herb or a diet to enable her to lose weight!

Naturopathy often consists of a brief and simple look at physics, chemistry, mechanics, meteorology ('wind' is called 'meteorism' in the best medical texts), geology (for the mineral needs) and biochemistry, to understand how humans fit in with all the other natural science laws. No wonder ancient Egyptian physicians and surgeons were also trained in botany, agriculture, astronomy, biology, physics, chemistry, 'psychology', and the art of educating patients, as a teacher of natural laws.

'Lady,' I gently chided my patient, 'you're fat because you are permanently carrying around inside you two or three garbage-bins full of decaying rubbish.'

Too simple for a medical textbook? It made great sense to her, as did the laxatives and alteratives I prescribed first to clean her out; and following that the nerve and blood-supply toners, to restore natural peristaltic signals to the bowel and give her inertia-bound alimentary tract the first push towards a more balanced movement pattern.

One of the prime obstacles a naturopath must overcome when treating the organs of elimination, is the way that basic personality-editing we call 'education', or 'growing up' causes us to cling to all sorts of elimination processes. When we were small we were not allowed to tell father he smelt rotten from smoking cigarettes and drinking alcohol and we didn't want a hug from a smelly drunk. All through life we hang on to material possessions, other people, money, security, hate, resentment, and territory. Eliminating out-grown attitudes, bad emotional partnerships, inappropriate jobs, even old, worn-out clothing, can be difficult for many human beings, and the longer they refuse to give these things up, the sicker they become.

Many kinds of rubbish, not only faeces, contribute to illnesses with far more serious prognoses than constipation! Metabolic waste products provide an ideal breeding-ground nutritionally, where random and abnormal cells proliferate and then infiltrate be moved through the first leg of its elimination journey as far as the bowels.

The three-way causative factors of illness apply more to the bowels than to any other organ or function: circumstantial and emotional 'hang-on' to what the patient knows is unsatisfactory and negative can make you sicker quicker!

An elderly patient who had been a professional soldier was a sad example of this. He stomped in, upright and fierce, and spat at me, 'Got bowel cancer. Haven't let it get to me. Haven't changed a thing in the daily routine I've done all my life. Up at six, down at ten; three hearty meals every day; can still drink with the best of them and I've never let emotions stand in the way of duty.

Don't intend to start now.' He asked me for herbal laxatives. 'Always kept the bowels open all me life,' he boasted. 'Took paraffin every day, and if that didn't work, took mineral salts – buckets! Terribly important to keep the bowels functioning.'

It's doubtful whether, with that acquired personality, his bowels would *ever* have opened unless vigorously – and damagingly – thumped daily.

I often find that Valerian, which has absolutely no laxative properties at all, produces easy, natural, relaxed bowel-movements in such over-controlled, over-rigid, even self-righteous people. It is not just the colon but the *attitudes* that need to change and relax, to allow for human frailty as well as its courage and will power.

An excellent Bach remedy has a similar effect on the over-controlled, dominant, inflexible patient who issues orders about what he or she expects the naturopath to provide.

Another patient answered every question I put to him with 'Perfect!'

'How's your sleep pattern?'

'Perfect!'

'How's your handling of stress and emotional climate?'

'I don't let things like that interfere with my plans for my life,' he said with an icy stare.

'How are your bowels?'

'Perfect! Regular as clockwork every day of my life!'

His irises showed the dark brown-black spokes of Radii Solaris all around, emanating from a comparatively *clean* bowel zone. He died four months later of bowel cancer. Earlier there seemed to be nothing medically wrong that could be detected, nor had he complained about anything. But as soon as I saw those tell-tale dark spokes in the iris, I knew he had at least the *capacity* to self-destruct, not from the cause of obvious physical elimination symptoms, but because of the need to eliminate two other cause-factors from his life: his continuing marriage to a woman he hated violently, and his refusal to accept that this relationship may have had something to do with the tension headaches, about which he had consulted me.

'No business of yours what my marriage is like!' he snapped, when I finally winkled the real story out of him. 'Just fix my headaches!'

'I can't,' I answered him.

This brings me to another dictum of my grandmother's: 'Children need to keep their mouths shut and their bowels open,' she dictated to my mother. Then she winked at me. 'Come over here and talk to me about everything, and you won't have to face cascara syrup for constipation *ever*', she grinned. How I loved her for it and she was right!

It is not coincidental that many functions of the head are subtended above the transverse colon zone on the iris map. These days a medical diagnosis of 'constipation headache' is seldom handed out, but the wisest of wise old medical professors in the 1900s taught that major improvement in spirits, in energy, in thinking and concentration could be expected when constipation was removed.

The laxatives used then are the same as those on our clinic dispensary shelves today: cascara, aloes, liquorice and senna. These are all-powerful improvers of the bowel's capacity to 'think' for itself again, not just constant supports which daily will produce an apparent result, but real 'educators' of the bowel in what it *ought* to be doing on its own.

Figs, prunes, dates, molasses – all foods which are excellent natural improvers of bowel function

All herbal laxatives are high in iron and phosporus, and some in silica and sulphur as well: all are minerals which a naturally-eliminating bowel possesses in abundance. Foods which are excellent natural improvers of bowel function are figs, dates, grapes, dried raisins and currants and muscatels, molasses, plums and prunes. The black of liquorice and cascara extracts tells the same story, as does molasses. Nature has put up the landmarks again – the pointers to the rules – in her colour-coding. Black iron, black molasses and dark grape skins, black currants, blackish-brown faecal matter, and that black hole of Calcutta through which putrid, dead and decaying matter is removed from you.

Observation will tell you what the rules are, not the latest 'cure' for cancer, or a 'high fibre' diet, or even the newest 'scientific discovery' that Masai tribesmen excrete a greater volume of faecal matter than we do, therefore perhaps we too should live only on cow's milk and bull's blood, in order to 'cure' cancer of the bowel! Every week, it seems, another article or academic paper appears, concentrating *only* on the physical symptoms of ill-health, with virtually not a word on its *causes*.

All right: so far in this section we have explained not only *what* your bowels are doing, but *why* they are doing it. If that last-mentioned patient had answered my question about empty-ing the bowels slightly differently with, 'Oh, they're fine! Every time I have a good meal I go easily – at least twice a day, sometimes more', and my inspection of the iris had showed a clear, clean, undiscoloured, active intestinal tract, I *would* have taken that patient's word for it. That third law of motion I men-tioned earlier had been obeyed: 'action and re-action are equal and opposite'. Some in, and some out; the tides do it, the seasons do it, human cells do it. How can any rational, intelligent human believe that *not* doing it can be got away with scot-free?

Adrenalin flooding through the bloodstream when 'fight or flight' triggers arise, can have a powerful effect on the bowels. Every soldier knows 'trench-diarrhoea', and what does the hunted animal do when cornered, or the blow-fly on the window before the swat descends? It defaecates – urgently!

Constipation is certainly not the only abnormal bowel pattern! Too loose, too rapid motions when excretion is over-done alto-gether, upset the balance in another way. Input of any kind which presents a massive challenge – fear, panic, apprehension, anxiety – causes adrenal flooding, and the body responds immediately to remove as much of the stress as quickly as possible. This time, the physical component reacts to save the emotional and circumstantial ones from overwhelming the organism. Life's marvellous, isn't it? If any action or movement is made, an opposite reaction is ready to balance it!!

Constant running diarrhoea, in diseases like cholera, typhoid and dysentery, kills by emptying the bowels so rapidly that the whole body is destroyed by dehydration. Watch the pendulum in the grandfather clock: it swings back and forth, the same distance in the *same* time, in action and reaction movements. Tip it more *either* way, even with a feather-touch, and the balance will be destroyed.

Homeostasis, man's ability to balance his ups with downs, his ons with offs, his work with play, his emotional outlets with emotional feeding, and his physical bowels with physical food and nutrient intake, is a state where health is maintained unassisted by outside agents. The ability is for the organism to *regulate itself*.

Ask that bowel habit question with a different emphasis: not, 'Are you regular?', but 'Are you *regulating*?' Is your output consistent with your input? If you fast for five days, you should expect little excretion on the sixth. If you gorge on junk foods, heavy animal protein, empty carbohydrates, and fats and alcohol together, you can expect *major* elimination. If you're experiencing the former input but not the latter output, trouble lies ahead, and no amount of supportive vitamin pills or miracle pharmaceutical drugs will do anything to balance the chronic imbalance you're maintaining.

I could become awfully technical about 'clay-coloured stools', 'pelleted' faeces, black-hard solid impactions, steatorrhea and so on, but the simple truths of naturopathy remain: not only is the liver your chemical factory but it sorts your emotions as well. If whatever comes in in food – and emotions! – is good and appropriate, then whatever comes out will be simple and lacking complications, too. If your gall-bladder is storing resentment, as well as too much bile, faecal matter will be affected. If your nervous system is too exhausted to get you out of bed in the morning, your bowel won't receive accurate signals, either, to tell you when it wants to move, to excrete your 'sins' against natural (not Divine) laws.

Illnesses caused by inefficient excretion are amongst the most easily avoided ones, and are the most readily correctable *in the early stages*. Lifelong elimination difficulties result inexorably in major terminal diseases.

Now you can see why so many naturopaths start at the bottom end when talking health! The only quarrel I have with such doctrines is that of the 'shock' effect that even a good, but *too-sudden* change can produce. Many patients suffer great discomfort when elimination is too brisk, and haste can be dangerous. It takes a long time to establish unbalanced patterns of excretion; according to nature's laws it will – and should – take time to re-establish balance and a better pattern.

Many too-eager naturopaths rush into professional consultations (and also into print) with the same *wrong* philosophy that propelled the patient into ill-health in the first place, and has also brought down public condemnation on the heads of orthodox practitioners and their 'miracle' drugs; it takes *time* to get sick and *time* to become well-balanced again. There are no short-cuts which produce *lasting* effects, only short-term relief of symptoms. All those *cause*-factors need to be changed before a lasting restoration of balance is achieved.

I often have to tell a prospective patient, 'If you had come in twenty, or even ten years ago, we could have given you lasting, positive change; now, your body's balancing mechanisms will *never* be able to go it alone again, but will need constant, therapeutic intrusion even to keep them 'running on the spot', let alone to gain real improvement. Unfortunately, orthodox medicine opines: 'you must wait until you're really sick before a doctor can do anything to help you.' By that time, it may be far too late to do anything towards permanent correction.

In the main, naturopaths are educated to spot the earliest signs of illness-attack patterns and to head them off at the pass, not wait until there is a major all-out war! Nature tells you in hundreds of small ways, 'Go back, you are going the wrong way' (just as do those red freeway signs) *before* you find your bicycle is on a collision course with a ten-tonne truck!

The kidneys

Bowels are only one of the organs of elimination. The kidneys, the skin, and even the lungs, all help. Bowel walls allow water

The urinary system

The kidneys and the bladder are also important organs of elimination.

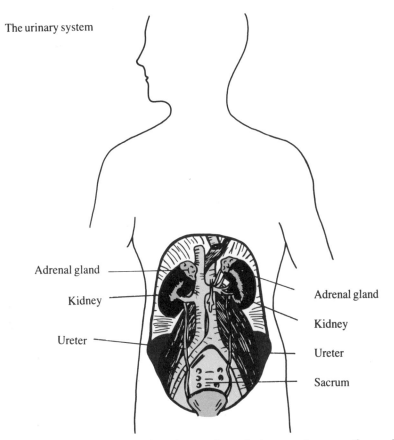

Adrenal gland

Kidney

Ureter

Adrenal gland

Kidney

Ureter

Sacrum

and a few other specialised protein substances to pass through them and back into tissues, eventually to be removed by the fluid-waste controllers, the kidneys. Like rainwater in drainage gutters, fluid wastes drain downhill, so your kidneys give you a nudge forward into the bladder reservoir and out, during the upright posture of daily activities.

At night, the excretion rate of the kidneys slackens off while you're horizontal in sleep. It is not only the pressurisation that plays up with your kidneys and gives you swollen, puffy ankles on long plane flights; it's sleeping (or trying to!) in an *upright* position instead of in a horizontal one. If I have a seat where it's possible to lie flat on the cabin floor or across three seats on a straight-through-to-London flight, my ankles don't swell. If I'm stuck in a seated position for some thirty hours or so, they do.

In the iridology chart, legs, ankles and feet are adjacent to the kidney zones.

One of the first signs of chronic kidney inefficiency is the 'tree-leg' look, where legs show little shape and ankles are almost as big as thighs, with feet painfully crammed into footwear, and overflowing! (Iridology iris-maps confirm not only anatomical partnerships and functional relationships, but overload directions when a particularly high loading is placed on any part of the body, the mind, or the emotions.)

Kidneys removing fluid waste-products must also accommodate great variation in fluid pressures. Together with blood-stream fluids and lymphatic fluids they must continually regulate the liquid excretion without emptying you completely or allowing you to overfill.

Using herbal diuretics

The class of chemical compounds called 'diuretics' are prescribed for the commonest side of the fluid imbalance to be found in people who live in affluent countries: overfilling. All diuretics, whether pharmaceutical or herbal, use potassium compounds to remove excess fluids from cells. All *herbal* diuretics, however, contain a balance of the other nutrients needed to maintain the sodium *'in'* and the potassium *'out'* pumping action. Celery, for instance, is high in sodium with some potassium; juniper berries are high in potassium with some sodium as well. Herbal diuretics raise both sodium and potassium levels so that the cellular pump-action improves both ways, taking a continual uphill load off the kidneys.

Naturopathy does not assume that man can improve on what was a theoretically perfect fluid pumping-station at birth, only that he should attempt to support its excellent efficiency if and when it fails for lack of proper or appropriate maintenance.

Naturopathy, in its theory and practice, is a *maintenance modality*. Don't wait until something goes wrong before it is serviced and repaired! Regular maintenance *prevents* breakdown and the early wearing out of parts, keeping everything in good condition. Celery in the diet, juniper berries tea, can be household ways of maintaining your kidneys' efficiency. So can rolled oats and asparagus, dandelion leaves in salads, and most other salad vegetables.

'Salads are nothing but water!' complained one patient in his late forties who had asked us for some 'natural' diuretic pills to replace the pharmaceutical ones he'd been taking. (He didn't fancy at all several of the latter's side-effects, especially impotence!) 'You mean I should just eat rabbit's-food to keep my blood pressure down and my kidneys working better? Surely salads will *add* more water?'

Nature has it all balanced for us again; not just water, but the two minerals needed to flush out clogged-up pumping-station machinery and clear the mains pressure are all built into those healthful salads!

Any job which ought to be done by the kidneys, but which is not carried out, will result in 'dirty' blood returning to the heart. Diuretics are often prescribed medically for patients with heart symptoms, whereas, in naturopathy, the idea *always* is to maintain all the organs or structures at maximum efficiency to avoid that progressive pattern of overload jumping from first one culprit to another and yet another organ or structure. Small day-to-day adjustments avoid the necessity for later major stripping-down and repair work.

Most salad vegetables are essential for regular 'maintenance', and keep those elimination organs in good running order.

Never ignore a full bladder

Many patients seem inordinately proud of their ability to hold their urine. The fragility of the human ego never ceases to astonish me! Even the pitiful boast of, 'I can go all day if I have to' seems to lift many a self-image!

'Your kidneys and bladder can't,' I reply, rather deflatingly. The contents of the bladder begin to undergo chemical breakdown and change if stored too long, and the best way to irritate the lining of the bladder is not to 'go' when the contents need voiding.

The pressure of a full bladder puts strains on other organs in the pelvic zone, especially on reproductive organs and the lower bowel. Many an enlarged and inflamed prostate gland may have started twenty years earlier with unnecessary 'hanging on'! That early-morning bladder-pressure which sends you reluctantly from warm bed to cold bathroom is an urgent signal, strong enough to switch you from relaxation to action. Half the world is woken not by alarm clocks, but by full bladders!

Have you also noticed how the first morning urine is stronger, darker, and greater in quantity than any other? Your kidneys and bladder have been somewhat slowed down during parasympathetic sleep processes, otherwise you'd have been up every two or three hours during the night.

If you do have to get up two or three times in the night to urinate, you should suspect that your nervous system has not fully relaxed from action into rest. A person who sleeps poorly, who experiences broken rest and physical muscular tension, may *think* that their bladder woke them up, when actually the reverse was the case. They woke their bladder up! A nervous system which does not close down fully for the night can cause that daytime bladder pattern to continue; every few hours, your body will receive a signal from the bladder.

Are the reasons for bed-wetting now plainer? And why herbalists use nervines (plants which have a calming effect on the balance between conscious and automatic halves of the nervous system) to correct it? Sometimes chiropractic adjustment of the spine helps this distressing problem, too, or treatment with acupuncture balances nerve impulses which are inappropriate, but have become a habit.

One of my patients is a taxi-driver, a young woman in her

twenties who looked forty-five when first she consulted me regarding the dark circles under her eyes, her greyish, sallow, sagging skin, her foul breath, lower back pain and period problems, and poor sleep.

Bad naturopathic practice would have been to give her at least two different kinds of tablets for each symptom. *Good* naturopathic practice looks much more directly and simply at the whole: and her overall problem seemed to be poor elimination.

Her answers to my questions confirmed this. She hung on 'all day' in her cab because she had had a phobia about public lavatories since her childhood. Her bladder stayed full and over-full, and her bowels were in a like condition, sometimes for twelve to sixteen hours at a time, while she ignored all signals to 'go'. It was no surprise to me when she later confessed to chronic cystitis, and even an occasional 'accident' when tired. She urinated four or five times at night, and suffered from broken sleep. It's predictable that her foul breath and unattractive skin (the only two organs left in her whole elimination system!) were the result.

I insisted that she 'go' when her nervous system demanded; she insisted public lavatories were 'too nasty'. No amount of information on clean, attractive, 'safe' lavatories in hotels, public buildings, even shops and restaurants, would sway her: she still requested 'natural' treatment.

Well, I told her, she'd had it! There is no way any 'physical' treatment can overcome the other two components of nature, environment and emotions, if the human will is implacably fixed.

When I last heard, she had discovered a 'natural' toothpaste for bad breath, and a 'natural' cosmetic to remove the dark circles under her eyes, and she was full of words about the 'incompetence' of 'that naturopath'! Our profession needs to acquire thick skins early on!

Children and bowel habits

Many Victorian-era attitudes towards excretion survive in our so-called enlightened age. Children who otherwise would excrete from bowel and bladder quite happily as part of their bodies' natural function often have the 'dirty' aspect of the elimination system drummed into them early. Sure, there is an abundance of bacteria in there: all the more reason for those waste products to be *out* of the body. It should be an occasion for rejoicing when bowels and bladder empty. But too many children are still confronted with a 'potty' and some form of disapproval follows if their body signals do not tell them to 'go' right there and then.

Mum or Grandma feels a failure if their child is not 'trained' earlier than the neighbour's baby or at whatever age the currently popular authority states is necessary.

Show a young child very early in the piece their dirty or wet nappy and the lavatory-available-when-you-feel-like-that-again routine. If *you* act out a sit-on-the-toilet-to-excrete game, a child will learn as everything else is learned – by imitation, experience, and an understanding of the natural process and its signals *beforehand*.

There's nothing so damaging to a child's later 'wholth' as an adult than turning the processes of excretion into a battleground. (It's even worse than that other grievance area and destroyer of so many digestive systems, the family dinner table.) Why on earth do we continue to enact that tableau of a determined adult, jaw set, glaring at a small, enthroned child and challenging, 'You'll just stay there until you *do* it!' Fewer nappies to wash? A necessity to establish who is master? There is nothing like this sort of challenge to make an anal sphincter or a bladder jam tight *shut*.

Allow a child's natural gift for mimicry to be the stimulus. You can certainly help by carefully observing when some excretion is likely, and playing the lavatory game then. But insisting that small children sit, like recruits in dog-obedience classes, at times when sitting does not come naturally, has resulted in generations of constipated, 'holding-on' adults.

Skin: the third kidney

Many of those overweight people who regulate their solid food intake in different dietary regimes, yet lose no weight at all, are retaining fluids. A large number of such people lead sedentary existences in which hard physical work or exercise is not part of their day.

One elimination organ can be greatly helped by the support of another. The lungs and the skin can also be called organs of excretion. The skin is often called 'the third kidney', and it has the greatest surface area in the body, which makes it ideal for fluid excretion.

The skin is often called the third kidney. Working up a sweat can give your kidneys a holiday and then a tonic!

Perspiration means 'skin-breathing'. Working up a sweat can give your kidneys a holiday and then a tonic! Surprisingly large amounts of fluid can be lost in hard labour or vigorous exercise.

Just as massage or exercise can push the lymphatic circulation harder, so it can also activate the skin itself into major elimination activity, as can a sauna or a brisk rub with a skin-brush before a bath. Whatever moves the skin about – even a smile – stimulates the process.

Sunshine on the skin also activates the lymphatic and general circulation, and produces those runnels of sweat which can drain directly from major lymph collection points at throat, under arms and down the chest.

Sweating profusely when one has been working hard is a natural process; so is drinking a lot of water during work, or just afterwards, to replace and restore fluid balance again. If the skin is pushed into too strong an exercise of excretion, the kidneys can urgently need that water, as can the blood!

Using aromatic oils

The most marvellously direct way of replacing those waste products lost through the skin with brand-new nutrient material is with a cosmetic moisturiser containing that large class of herbal extractives, the aromatic oils. You can even put a few drops of the pure oil in bathwater to suit your mood or your workload: rosemary for muscle relaxation; lavender to calm nervous energy; cinnamon to help you stay awake and read or study; lemon as an astringent and antiseptic; and so the list goes on.

Rosemary oil in your bathwater will help muscle relaxation

For just as the skin excretes prolifically, it also absorbs well. First clean out the garbage, then feel the major effect of cosmetically-used nutrients. Save your mouth and your digestion the fuelling job!

One of France's greatest herbalists, Maurice Messegué, treated his patients mainly with hand and foot baths containing medicinal plant leaves, roots and flowers. These natural substances are not only pleasant to use, but are a pleasant means of gaining a major therapeutic effect. Cascara and foul brown smelly extracts to empty the bowels are not the only remedies. Your skin can reduce the workload on your kidneys and bowels. *Use* these natural balances and partnerships. Once you understand those immutable Laws of Nature you can make them work for you.

Lungs

Your lungs can join in the elimination round, also. If they exhale the carbon dioxide wastes and the stale end-products of our smog and pollution-laden air efficiently, most of these acid end-products pose far less of a threat to us than the morning haze over our cities and factories may suggest. If lungs are inefficient, and – worse still – incompletely cleared of carbon dioxide and wastes, your inhalation of even minor, air-borne irritants can be *more* dangerous than the pollution level readings might indicate. Health equals *efficiency* of operation!

Breathe in deeply, then exhale strongly, in order to begin

Efficient lungs help you overcome the adverse effects of our city smogs and pollution-laden air educating your lungs in breathing more efficiently. It sounds absurdly simple, but breathing well must be learned like every other skill. Did you raise your shoulders up in the air when you took in that deep breath? Inefficient! Better by far to pump your lungs from the *bottom* (that is, from the diaphragm) in order to expel wastes; don't hoist them up from the shoulder-girdle.

Gravity puts solid and liquid waste material at the *bottom* of lungs. Many people who breathe incorrectly use only the top half, or even third, of their lung capacity at each breath. If you do this, it is no wonder you feel tired! When you breathe this way, the amount of oxygen available to you is equivalent to being halfway up a high mountain. There's more about oxygen in the respiratory chapter, but the elimination function of your lungs is more than half the story of breathing efficiency.

'Exertion asthma' can be the diagnosis when energetic activity provokes coughing and wheezing. Exhalation starts to clear much waste material and occludes these air passages. Educate your lungs! Yoga breathing is one way; walking briskly is another; so is swimming and many other forms of regular two-sided exercise like bicycling or rowing. Much of the health of trained sportsmen and women can be attributed to their efficiency in breathing and in excreting wastes.

How clean is your four-section rubbish removal system? Solid, liquid and gas: it all needs throwing away *completely* as fast as it builds up.

Wastes of many different kinds make ideal 'food' and breeding grounds in which abnormal cells may proliferate. Everyone is born with some abnormal cells, random cells, imperfect cells; whether these are given food and sustenance depends on how efficiently elimination organs remove the waste products of human metabolism from their reach.

Don't forget those other two members of the illness-producing trinity: environmental wastes and emotional wastes. Throw out the job that's killing your nervous system or the worn-out emotions that are ruining your love-life. Abandon those rigidly-held attitudes that prevent you learning new and better ways. Regular emptying leaves room for new filling! Certainly, retain those feelings, attitudes and circumstances that provide you with satisfaction and 'wholth', but nothing fresh, new and stimulating can enter unless you discard those worn-out bits of you and your life.

10   *Finale*

IF YOU bought this book to find out how many grams of vitamin C are the rule for curing colds, you will have been disappointed. There are no good diets in it, either! But if you now understand what a vastly complex array of inter-reacting cells and systems you are, perhaps you'll be wondering how the balance is maintained as well as it usually is.

Your body, which contains your mind and your emotions as well as the physical components of specialised cells and functioning, moving parts, is self-regulating to an amazing degree. Understanding how all these interlocking and compensating systems work is the first step towards monitoring and maintaining its healthy function.

If you now understand that the pain in the neck you are consulting your naturopath about is caused by your mother-in-law's effect on your health, you may not be so quick to demand an appropriate amount of calcium orotate to correct it! If your particular allergy flares at the end of every year, it may not only be caused by the flowering privet or pollens, but the onset of examinations and their effect on your parasympathetic nervous system. If you bitterly resent the raw deal life has given you, don't be surprised when gallstones are found on your X-rays.

That three-way reason for ill health is one of nature's most immutable laws: how you feel, and how you interact with your environment are always 'sick' too when there is *physical* ill-health present. Cancer can be triggered off by despair as well as by carcinogenic substances, or, as a recent English 'Foundation' of yet another kind found, by unemployment and the sudden shock of job loss. Even that broken leg would not have happened if you hadn't been in a tearing rush after a quarrel or a frustrating morning with the children. One of the biggest blunders committed by science and orthodox medicine was when they decided that the physical symptoms *only* needed treatment.

'What about psychiatry?' I can hear you saying defensively. The practice of psychiatry insists that only your mind is sick. In this branch of medicine the other two components, the physical and the environmental, are ignored! Until medicine treats the whole patient again, and recognises the interaction of feelings and circumstances with the physical body as a unit the whole of which is sick, true health care will not return.

An efficient, three-way function produces excellent health. Every facet of your living experience needs polishing, not just your vitamin intake! Of course, good food and improved nutrition is part of it all, but so is explaining that you cannot hope for your stomach pains to improve, no matter how good your diet, if fear and tension are constant table-companions, and you hate the expensive dining-room table that you really couldn't afford!

Having chosen 'wholistic' medicine, the best way to begin your return to real health lies in seeking a professional naturopathic opinion *first*. You may or may not agree with what you are told, but at least your practitioner will have studied the subject more than you. The time to begin 'doing it yourself' is *after* you have found out accurately what needs to be done.

Many of the diagnostic methods your naturopath will use are as old as the hills. Some of them have not been recognised for centuries, but are now proving to have valid and 'scientific' reasons for re-use. It is not so long ago that acupuncture was rubbished by orthodox medicine as 'backward country non-sense'. Later, after seeing incontrovertible proof of its effectiveness, many medical doctors began to use it as an alternative to orthodox therapies. Why? Because it works!

Iridology, known in 4000 BC in Egypt, and AD 500–600 in what was then Palestine, re-surfaced this century in Germany and then in North America. Its protagonists were subjected to the same ridicule as were the acupuncturists in the 1950s. A highly-respected reconstructive surgeon said to my husband just recently, 'If it's being rubbished vociferously it *must* be good!' He spoke from bitter experience. His own out-in-front developments in reconstructive surgery have made him a vilified and ridiculed figure amongst his own medical fraternity. His patients know better! Nowhere is radical change feared and resisted more than in orthodox medicine.

Iridology and acupuncture are old as well as new; so is hygiene, believe it or not! Hygea and Panacea, the daughters of Asklepios, may or may not have existed in fact. But writings of the period talk about washing the hands before eating and after defecating. Oils and extracts were rubbed on the body to deodorise it and to prevent bacterial infections, long before the word, bacteria, was invented. Spa-baths and saunas were used in ancient Rome and mediaeval Scandinavia. Herbal teas have been drunk since recorded history. Two or three generations ago, cod liver oil was popped down every British child's throat, and sulphur and molasses too! So what is new and radical about 'wholistic' medicine?

Now comes the punch-line. 'Alternative' medicine is not alternative at all! It's straight-line medicine, and it always has been, a direct continuum of the arts and understanding practised for centuries.

Sure, we have made some improvements: we no longer flail the back with stinging nettles to treat low blood pressure. But present-day German naturopaths still apply leeches frequently, and with the same age-old results: to relieve bruising and congestion by 'letting blood'. We don't exorcise the 'evil' from the body by incantations and spells, but we do advise 'positive thinking' and 'attitude reinforcement', which can have a powerful physiological effect. Even the word 'quack', if you go back to its origins, has nothing to do with silly old ducks who happen to be naturopaths! The name derives from quicksilver, or mercury (from the Dutch quacksalver), which was first used in medical treatment of syphilis.

Henry VIII grew tired of the feuds between the Barbers' Guild and the Surgeons' Guild, and granted a Charter which is a fine example of post-Solomonian logic and wisdom. This states that whoever has knowledge of the cultivation and use of plants should use them for treatment, and whoever has knowledge of surgery should use this means when necessary. There was no 'official recognition', the catch-phrase many politically-minded naturopaths bandy about as if they were second-class citizens medically! The patients were the final arbiters.

If 'cures' were effected, that practice grew. If cures were *not* effected, and/or exorbitant fees were charged, the practice shrank. We can see that happening again in medicine, right now.

Naturopaths all, hold your heads up and don't assume you have to beg orthodoxy to recognise how valid your art is in philosophy and practice.

This brings us to the present, but what about the future? Where lies the trail ahead in naturopathy?

I often plead with naturopaths to keep it all *simple*. There is a rough and rocky road ahead if a visit to a naturopath results in typed sheets detailing what to do every hour of the day, rigid instructions about what to eat and drink, and an expensive series of allergy tests, water filters, cartons of tablets and the practitioner's autocratic insistence on 'no sins at all'! Nature's rules are flexible within limits; only if you step outside the guidelines altogether do you suffer the inevitable consequences. Let your patients be human! Don't replace the strict black and white of scientific medicine with an even more rigid grey of naturopathic complication. Remember those balance pans on the scales! A *little* is all that is needed to start the swing going the other way.

Homoeopathy recognises this principle as the 'minimum dose'. If you have experienced homoeopathic treatment, you will know the massive and powerful effect it is possible to achieve by using the tiniest, almost infinitesimal, dose of any substance. Don't overtreat as naturopaths. Don't hitch your patients up to machines or baffle them with authority and an almost manic intensity on adherence to your rules. After all, this is why your patients have become dissatisfied with orthodox medical and surgical treatment. Don't fall into the same trap!

New and exciting fields are opening up in naturopathic

diagnostic techniques. Hair analysis, radiesthesia, tongue and ear diagnosis (which the Chinese have used for centuries), aura measuring, colour therapy, etc., all have come from the past, and all show promise for use in the future. Postural analysis helps locate those structurally mis-aligned spots which put abnormal strains on tissues in the same area.

Science now possesses the fine and delicate measuring instruments which can validate (if you still feel it necessary) the fact that your aura glows redly when you suffer the emotion of anger, or inflammation of the body tissues, or when you are struggling to overcome the panic experienced by physical attack. So what's new? Red has always signified danger, of one kind or another. Red blood flowing; a red face in extreme heat or activity; red veins in the whites of the eyes; even the old rhyme about the weather – 'red sky in the morning'. Red traffic lights and a red-coated soldier tell us the same story.

Are you growing to understand the simple story of naturopathy? Nature's signs are easy to read, and similar signs mean similar processes, even when Science and Civilisation try to copy. *Observation* is the key to it all.

The 'magic' or 'witchcraft' label really needs to be dropped. So does the word 'primitive', when natural diagnosis and natural therapies are discussed. No elite group of enlightened magicians works at superhuman and even impossible things! I teach my students that there is no need to superimpose the words 'magic' or 'mystical' if you take the trouble to *observe* and *find out*. Maybe genius is 10 per cent inspiration and 90 per cent perspiration, but naturopathy is 10 per cent rationalisation of the 90 per cent of observation preceding it. It's all there if you spend time reading the signs!

So those who've studied geomagnetism and quantum theory, acoustics and colour vibrations, astronomy and astrophysics, may be naturopathy's new running partners. 'As above, so below', applies to a wave cycle of sound just as much as to a metaphysical philosophy. The energy-measuring sciences will do more to 'validate' naturopathy in years to come than will any application for registration and recognition.

It has already been found that cells 'sing' a note which raises harmonies in other cells and cause an energy flow to begin. Abnormal tissue gives off abnormal 'sounds', just as the iris records colour and structure changes in different disease or health conditions. Laws of Nature which apply to human matter, as they do to any other combination of chemistry and physics, exist already.

Research in our own clinic has led us to a conclusion which has been long known and recognised by horticulturists and animal breeders. A huge percentage of physical, mental and environmental diseases and dissatisfactions is your ancestors' fault, not yours. Orthodox medicine has totally ignored the old 'miasms', or genetic 'ghosts' of diseases like leprosy, scrofula, syphilis and tuberculosis, which theoretically have been 'cured', but in practice have never been totally removed.

We have found many of the allergies, skin diseases, mental and personality disorders and the unpredictable periodicity of many disease symptoms to be ancestral and genetic 'ghosts' of past diseases. Plant and animal geneticists accept this principle as mundane: applied to people, however, eyebrows rise in shock and trigger memories of 'racial purity' and purges.

It is a fact, however, that sick parents will breed sick children, probably along a different disease track in accordance with the Mendelian principle. However, do you think you should be optimistic about the future if your irises are murky, your skin is greenish-coloured and your general health is not as good as one should expect? If you do follow all the right natural, simple and commonsense measures from here on in, your children and your grandchildren will be genetically better off, and they will there-fore be subjected to less of a burden from their adverse ancestral inheritance.

It can all start with you! Find out all about yourself from a naturopath. (Every person will be different.) Take the pro-fessional advice and treatment, if your instincts tell you it all makes sense, then continue at home and everyday, using your simple knowledge of how the collection of cells called a human being works. If you take steps to avoid the first processes of disease, then the terminal processes need not happen. And look to your living conditions; your job, your household, your envir-onment, not forgetting the emotional 'poisons' in attitudes of mind and personality.

Good health to you in every sense of the word!

194

Acknowledgements

The author and publishers would like to acknowledge the following for permission to use illustrations and quoted matter. Every effort has been made to contact sources of material, but occasionally we were unsuccessful. The publishers would be pleased to learn of any omission.

Vision Press and Peter Owen, for the figure drawing on page 3, from *The Human Figure* by David K. Rubins; The Book of Herbs by Dorothy Hall, published by Angus & Robertson, was the source of the line illustrations of herbs on pages 2, 4, 12, 15, 34, 54, 58, 61, 68, 73, 76, 89, 111, 126, 135, 153, 167, 185, 188; Michael Edgeley International, for the photograph of the Mechakarov Troupe on page 35 and Komlos of the International Circus on page 36; News Limited, for photograph on page 43; BBC Hulton Picture Library, for photograph page 69; Telecom Australia, for photograph page 70; Childbirth Education Association (Vic.) and the family, for the photograph on page 77; the Melbourne *Herald*, for photographs pages 80, 81; United Press International, for photograph page 90; The Melbourne *Herald*, for photograph page 96; Professor R. Twidale, for photograph page 99; News Limited, for photograph page 100; the Anti-Cancer Council of Victoria, for extract from their brochure on smoking and lung cancer, page 83 and illustrations of BSE, page 105; the NSW Cancer Council, for extract from their brochure on breast cancer, page 105; the Melbourne *Herald*, for photograph page 109; Lynn and Reid Preston and Kicks Health Centre, for photograph page 110; the Melbourne *Herald*, for photographs pages 117, 125, 127 and 130; the St John Ambulance Brigade, for photograph page 131; BWD Electronics, for photograph top 138; the Melbourne *Herald*, for photograph page 138 (foot); Community Welfare Services Department, for photograph page 140; the Australian Broadcasting Corporation, for photograph page 142; the Melbourne *Herald*, for photograph page 145; the Salvation Army, for photograph page 147; United Press International, for photograph page 149; McElroy & McElroy and United International Pictures Pty, for still from *The Year of Living Dangerously* on page 157; the Melbourne *Herald*, for photographs pages 158, 161; Victorian Autistic Children's and Adults' Association, for photograph page 162; the Australian Broadcasting Corporation, for photograph page 166; Lynn and Reid Preston and Kicks Health Centre, for photograph page 185; the Melbourne *Herald*, for photograph page 186.

Cover photography was by Tandey Rowley of Sydney; black and white step-by-step photography of chiropractic techniques, cranial-osteopathic techniques and naturopaths at work was by David Liddle, Sydney.

Index

THE NATURAL HEALTH BOOK
by Dorothy Hall

This guide to health through sensible eating stresses the virtues of freshly-grown foods and a natural diet. Dorothy Hall believes that every human being is an individual and must be treated as a whole person; that it is important to discover each body's needs and supply them. Then we may attain the happy state that is natural health – our bodies working efficiently, immune to trivial ills, so that we can forget about them and get on with the business of living our lives to the full.

The author explains clearly what the various vitamins and minerals do in the body, which ones occur in which foodstuffs, how they keep us healthy and active when properly balanced, and what ills the lack of any one element can cause.

Dorothy Hall classes good, bad and indifferent foods by their nutritional values (with some warnings about the quality and processing of refined and packaged foods), and she points out why some foods may be good for some people, but bad for others.

There are sections on instinctive eating, the whys and wherefores of organic growing, the use of wild plants and weeds in our gardens as foods and as medicines, the simple home remedies our grandmothers used; they all round out this commonsense handbook so rich in useful and unusual information. Based on scientific research and clinical observation, this book could change for the better the lives of many who read it; for it explains how may health problems may be *prevented* through good nutrition.

THE NATURAL HEALTH COOKBOOK
by Dorothy Hall

Are you trying to do the right thing by your own and your family's good health? Are you baffled by food combinations, dietary regimes and conflicting opinions on what to eat and how to prepare it? Are you ready to give up and buy take-aways?

Don't despair! THE NATURAL HEALTH COOKBOOK shows how ordinary recipes can become nutritionally rich; and offers hundreds more which are not only appetising but show you countless ways of preparing 'good' food to suit the individual nutritional needs of your home group. Each vitamin and mineral you need for efficient functioning has its own section of recipes for healthy meals, drinks and snacks.

With this valuable book you can learn about the health patterns and food requirements of each member of your household and discover why the same foods may not be right for everyone.

IRIDOLOGY
by Dorothy Hall

Can you say that you feel *really* healthy? Few people can. Do you
feel under par without knowing why? There's one way of
checking – through your eyes!

This straight-forward guide to the little-known subject of iridology
shows you how to interpret health and personality by looking
closely at the iris. Every part of your body relates to a section of
the iris, which can help pinpoint problems and imbalances.
Your nutritional pattern, your occupation, even your mental and
emotional state record themselves in the iris.

Dorothy Hall, an experienced practitioner, shows you how to
recognise the signs, dealing with each iris section in detail.
She explains the significance of iris colours, textures, patterns
and marks with reference to specific case histories and
easy-to-follow diagrams.

Use this book to see how your lifestyle is affecting your health.
Through iridology, you can find your own pattern of good health
and well-being – a pattern that is as distinctive and individual for
each of us as our fingerprints.